George Hess

History of the Antietam National Cemetery

Including a Descriptive List of all the Loyal Soldiers Buried therein

George Hess

History of the Antietam National Cemetery
Including a Descriptive List of all the Loyal Soldiers Buried therein

ISBN/EAN: 9783337307516

Printed in Europe, USA, Canada, Australia, Japan

Cover: Foto ©ninafisch / pixelio.de

More available books at **www.hansebooks.com**

HISTORY
OF THE
Antietam National Cemetery,
INCLUDING
A Descriptive List
OF ALL
The Loyal Soldiers Buried Therein:
Together with the Ceremonies
OF
ANCIENT, FREE AND ACCEPTED MASONS
IN
Laying the Corner-Stone of the
SOLDIER MONUMENT,
September 17th, 1867.

WRITTEN, ILLUSTRATED AND PUBLISHED BY
GEORGE HESS,
SUPERINTENDENT ANTIETAM NATIONAL CEMETERY.
LATE OF CO. I, 28TH REGT., PA. VET. VOL. INFANTRY.

HARRISBURG, PA.:
DAILY INDEPENDENT PRINT,
1890.

SUPERINTENDENT'S LODGE HOUSE.

CONTENTS.

	PAGE
A Patriotic Eagle at Camp Curtin, Pa., (Ill., Front Outside Cover),	
General Grant and his Brave Soldiers, (Ill., Back Outside Cover),	
George Hess, (Portrait),	2
Superintendent's Lodge House, (Ill.)	5
The Antietam National Cemetery,	7
Union Soldiers Graves on Antietam Battlefield, (Ill.)	10
Address of Governor Swann,	11
Large Monument, "Statuary," The American Soldier,	13
Programme of Ceremonies, Laying Corner-Stone of the Monument,	14
Extracts from the Oration of Ex-Governor Bradford,	20
Dedication Poem,	23
President Johnson's Speech,	28
Governor Geary's Speech,	29
Governor Fenton's Speech,	30
Order of Procession at Dedication of the Cemetery,	31
Programme of Arrangements at Dedication,	32
Oration of Abraham Lincoln at Dedication of Gettysburg National Military Cemetery,	33
Antietam National Cemetery, (Ill.)	34
Descriptive List of the Noble Dead, by States,	36
New York Section, Antietam National Cemetery, (Ill.)	62
Pennsylvania Section, Antietam National Cemetery, (Ill.)	96
Recapitulation of Names, by States,	128

THE ANTIETAM NATIONAL CEMETERY

IN March, 1865, the State of Maryland appropriated $7,000, and appointed four Trustees, viz.:

Augustine A. Biggs, of Sharpsburg, Md., President.
Thomas A. Boullt, of Hagerstown, Md., Secretary and Treasurer.
General Edward Shriver, of Frederick, Md.
Charles C. Fulton, of Baltimore, Md.

Said Trustees were instructed by the State of Maryland to purchase and inclose a suitable lot of ground on the battlefield of Antietam as a final resting place for the sacred remains of our brave soldiers who fell in that battle. Said Trustees at once entered upon the discharge of their duties. They purchased a suitable lot of ground in the suburbs of Sharpsburg, in sight of *Burnside Bridge, Dunkard Church, Headquarters of General McClellan and General Lee.* On this ground was the projection of a huge rock, upon which General Lee stood at intervals, where he could observe the movements of both the Federal and his own lines of battle, and issue orders to his corps and division commanders, until the advance of the Union Army drove him and his host beyond the town of Sharpsburg. (This rock has since been removed).

An act of the Maryland Legislature, March 23, 1865, that the expenses incident to the removal of the dead, enclosing and ornamenting the cemetery, etc., shall be appropriated among the States connecting themselves with the corporation, according to their population.

The appropriations made by the different States amounted to $62,229.77. In addition to the $7,000 appropriated by the State of Maryland, at its extra session in January, 1866, voted unanimously the additional appropriation of $8,000, thus making the sum altogether appropriated by her to the amount of $15,000.

The removal of the dead was commenced in October, 1866, by the United States Burial Corps, detailed by the General Government for the purpose, under the superintendence of Lieutenant John W. Shearer. This work was completed in August, 1867.

The local Trustees did not confine their action to the removal of the dead who fell at the battle of Antietam, but deemed it proper, at the suggestion of the authorities at Washington, to remove all the Federal dead who had been buried in Washington, Alleghany, and Frederick counties, Maryland. They were exhumed, placed in coffins, and delivered to the Superintendent, who buried them at the expense of the Association. Most of the Maryland dead, however, were removed by their friends immediately after the battle; also, Pennsylvania and other States removed a great many of their dead prior to the establishment of the National Cemetery.

In the burial of the dead every coffin was numbered, and a corresponding number entered in a book kept for this purpose, with the name, Company and State, when they could be ascertained, so that, at any time, by reference to the records, the location of any grave can at once be found. A peculiarity characteristic of this cemetery is, that a person occupying a position in the centre of the grounds (at monument) with his face turned to any point of the compass, can, with a good field glass, read the inscription on every headstone contained therein. The Cemetery is inclosed by a massive stone wall on three sides. This wall varies in height according to the slope of the ground, but on the inside a uniform height of 4 feet 3 inches below the coping, has been obtained by grading. In some places the wall is 12 to 16 feet high on the outside. The coping is 8 inches thick and 2 feet 5 inches wide; entire length of coping around the wall, 2,700 feet. On the north or front side there is a stone wall and coping about 3 feet high, surmounted by a neat and heavy iron fence. The wall and coping is built with gray limestone. The iron fence cost $6.00 per foot (lineal), of which there is about 600 feet. The main entrance is in about the centre of the iron fence and is closed by handsome iron gates, two drive and two foot, at a cost of $800.

The Cemetery itself is located on a gentle rise, from whence a survey of almost the entire battlefield may be enjoyed, while within the scope of the eye's range lies an unobstructed tract of country, miles in extent, taking in the distant South Mountain, memorable as the spot where the Confederate General Lee received his first check during the invasion of Maryland, and which caused him gradually to fall back with his army until it rested on the waters of the Antietam, and made a final stand only to be again defeated. In the far distance also looms up, in their majestic prominence, the continuous chain of the so-called Maryland Heights, rendered notorious as the rendezvous of John Brown prior to his raid on Harper's Ferry.

But a short distance from the foot of the Cemetery grounds flow the placid waters of Antietam, which gave its name to the conflict here waged, and which will be rendered memorable forever in story and in song.

The plan forms within the walls of the Cemetery a semi-ellipsis, divided into segments of circles, sections and parallelograms of varying size, to correspond with the number of the loyal dead from the different States represented in the battle, and each division is divided into sections of graves and numbered in order, and in States. That portion of the grounds devoted to this purpose begins at a point within about one hundred and thirty feet from the main entrance of the Cemetery. An arbor-vitae hedge, neatly trimmed and about 4½ feet high, forms a belt around the burial sections and bordering an eighteen-foot avenue, thus leaving a large open space between it and the wall, which extends along the line of the Sharpsburg and Boonsboro' pike in front. A main carriage drive, about 18 feet in width, leads from the entrance through the grounds, from which branches in different directions subordinate roads and walks leading to every part of the Cemetery, which are all well turfed with sod. The entire grounds are leveled to a uniform surface and well sodded, the grass being cut from three to four times a month during the growing season, making it look very beautiful at all times, and containing a thorough system of tube drainage, very complete, and which proves itself very valuable in maintaining good conditions against injury arising from heavy rains.

The grounds are also beautifully ornamented with the choicest assortment of evergreens, deciduous trees, and flower shrubbery.

Near the entrance to the Cemetery, and within the inclosure is a neat and commodious Lodge House, designed for the occupancy of the Superintendent of the Cemetery, with an office and reception room for the comfort and convenience of visitors.

Monuments.

In the centre of the grounds is erected a monument commemorative to the great event of the battle, and the heroism of those who sleep at its foot and around it. It is the colossal statue of an American soldier standing guard over the remains of the loyal dead, who are buried all around him, with this inscription on the die or shaft: "Not for Themselves, but for Their Country, Sept. 17th, 1862." This is the largest work of its kind in the country. The soldier stands twenty-two feet in height and the entire monument is forty seven feet high, weighing in all about 250 tons. The statue alone weighs twenty-nine tons. It is entirely of granite from the Westerly granite quarry at Westerly, R. I., and cost thirty thousand dollars.

Gun Monuments.

In passing up the main avenue, about a hundred feet from the entrance, are planted two iron guns, as monuments; the gun on the left is a 32-pound Columbiad, captured from the Confederates at Harper's Ferry (Bolivar Heights) by General Geary's men (28th Regiment P. V.) in 1861 and transported at once up the Chesapeake and Ohio canal to Williamsport, Md., and was brought from there to this spot in 1867. The gun on the right is a 12-pound rifled piece, was disabled near the foot of Elk Mountain (north) and about two miles east by north from the National Cemetery.

On the officers' section, near the Cemetery, and about a hundred and fifty feet due north of the large soldier monument, was erected in 1887, a neat and appropriate monument in memory of the fallen comrades who are buried in this Cemetery, by their surviving comrades of the 20th Regiment, N. Y. Vols. It is four feet six inches square at the base and nine feet high; on the second base or shaft, in front, is the following inscription: "20th Regiment N. Y. Vols. Turner Rifles, 3rd Brigade, 2nd Division, 6th Army Corps, 1861-1863." The statuary consists of a drum with regulation cap and corps badge, a wreath hanging over the drum; also belt with U. S. plate, cartridge box, bayonet scabbard, and canteen, hanging around on the drum. The entire monument is of granite from Westerly, R. I. Cost, eleven hundred dollars.

The dedication of the grounds to the sacred purposes for which they were designed, occurred on the fifth anniversary of the battle—the 17th day of September, 1867—at which time also was laid the corner-stone of the monument, with appropriate ceremonies.

Through the sacrifices and blood they shed, and the lives they rendered up, the Union has been preserved, our institutions are unimpaired, and our Government is strengthened; therefore, should we honor and keep green the memory of the loyal volunteer whose work has been accomplished, and the benefit of whose deeds and prowess as a nation we to-day enjoy.

UNION SOLDIERS' GRAVES ON ANTIETAM BATTLEFIELD.

The whole number of bodies interred in the Cemetery amount to 4,734, of which 2,869 are known, and 1,865 unknown, a number exceeding those interred in the Gettysburg Cemetery by 1,147. In the year 1877 the Cemetery was transferred to the United States Government and is now under its care and maintenance. The expenditure up to 1877 was in the neighborhood of one hundred thousand dollars. The cost and expenditure on the Cemetery at this time is estimated at sixteen hundred dollars per annum.

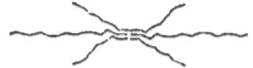

Address of Governor Swann.

The ceremonies were commenced by Governor Swann, who delivered a brief speech, which was cheered at the conclusion, as follows:

FELLOW COUNTRYMEN—Before proceeding with the programme, which has been handed me by the Committee of Arrangements, it seems appropriate that, as the official organ of the State of Maryland, upon whose soil and with whose hearty co-operation this Cemetery has been founded, I should extend a cordial welcome to His Excellency the President of the United States and his Cabinet the Governors of our sister States, and the distinguished guests who have come to participate in the ceremonies of this most interesting occasion.

During the administration of my immediate predecessor, the first appropriation was made by the State of Maryland towards establishing a burial place for the dead who fell upon the battlefield of Antietam.

At a subsequent period, the appropriation thus made having been found inadequate, upon the application of the Commissioners charged with this trust, a further sum was added in response to a communication made by myself to the Legislature in this behalf. Maryland having thus done her share in providing a burial place for these brave and patriotic men, the co-operation of our sister States was invoked to lend their aid in throwing around it a national interest, and the most liberal contributions have been accordingly made by nearly all the States in the removal of their dead, the erection of monuments, and in adding to the attractiveness of this beautiful spot. The work, so far as it has progressed, is now before you.

The flag which floats over us to-day is the flag of our Union. The sword of battle has been sheathed. The tramp of contending armies, the embittered strife of father against son, and brother against brother, no longer resounds within our borders. The star of this great Republic is again in the ascendant. In the calm sunshine of peace we are here to mingle our tears with the survivors of the illustrious dead who have sacrificed their lives for their country, and are sleeping upon this field.

May I not, in this solemn hour, invoke the interposition of Almighty God for a speedy restoration of harmony and brotherly love throughout this broad land; and that North, South, East and West, laying aside the animosities of the past, we may stand together hereafter, and in all future time, as one people, having a common origin and bound together by a common destiny? May this Union be perpetual.

Next followed prayer by Rev. Hiram Matison, D. D., of New Jersey. Then the hymn composed by Rev. Edward Meyer, was sung by the assemblage.

HYMN I.—*Old Hundred.*

"Aceldama!" O Lord, our God,
  Who evermore dost Israel keep,
Watered in tears, baptized in blood,
  Thou givest our beloved sleep.

They came at Freedom's trumpet call,
  From hall and cottage, fane and dome,
Venturing limb and life, and all
  For Truth and Right, for hearth and home!

Thousands of heroes bit the dust,
  Antietam, on thy crimson field!
Thrice armed were they, with quarrel just,
  The Lord their banner, sun and shield.

Lift high the granite shaft for all
  That fell where duty summoned them;
Their country's star-gem'd flag their pall,
  A Nation's wail their requiem!

O Lord! and shall they live again,
  These bones, the seed of crimson strife?
Thy Spirit breathes upon these slain,
  And they shall thrill with endless life.

In living hope, then, we commit
  This precious dust, for Freedom giv'n,
To thee, till angels gather it,
  Transfigured in the urn of Heav'n!

The corner-stone of the Monument was then laid according to Masonic rites.

Monument, "Statuary," The American Soldier.

PROGRAMME OF CEREMONIES

OF

Ancient, Free and Accepted Masons

WAS OBSERVED IN

LAYING THE CORNER-STONE

OF THE

MONUMENT

AT THE

Antietam National Cemetery,

AT SHARPSBURG, MD.,

TUESDAY, SEPTEMBER 17th, A. L. 5867,

*Which was laid by Most Worshipful JOHN COATES,
Grand Master of the Grand Lodge of Maryland.*

ORDER.

BAND OF MUSIC.

SUBORDINATE LODGES

OF A. F. AND A. MASONS.

CHAPTERS AND GRAND CHAPTERS.

PROGRAMME OF CEREMONIES.

COMMANDERIES AND GRAND COMMANDERIES.

VISITING GRAND LODGES.

BAND OF MUSIC.

THE M. W. THE GRAND LODGE OF MARYLAND.

GRAND TYLER, with drawn Sword.

GRAND DIRECTOR OF CEREMONIES AND GRAND PURSUIVANT.

THREE GREAT LIGHTS,

Carried by a Past Master.

SILVER PITCHERS, WITH OIL AND WINE,

Carried by Past Masters.

CORNUCOPIA,

Carried by a Past Master,

BOOK OF CONSTITUTIONS,

Carried by a Past Master.

GRAND CHAPLAIN.

PAST GRAND TREASURERS AND GRAND SECRETARIES.

R. W. GRAND TREASURER AND GRAND SECRETARY.

PAST JUNIOR AND SENIOR GRAND WARDENS.

R. W. JUNIOR AND SENIOR GRAND WARDENS.

PAST DEPUTY GRAND MASTERS.

R. W. DEPUTY GRAND MASTER.

PAST M. W. GRAND MASTERS.

| W. JR. G. DEACON, Jewel and Rod. | M. W. GRAND MASTER. | W. SR. G. DEACON, Jewel and Rod. |

GRAND SWORD BEARER.

TWO GRAND STEWARDS,

With White Rods,

CEREMONIES.

MUSIC BY THE BAND

OPENING.

M. W. Grand Master.—Right Worshipful Senior Grand Warden: The Grand Lodge of Maryland having been assembled for the purpose of Laying the Corner-Stone of the Monument, here to be erected, it is my order that the Most Worshipful Grand Lodge of Maryland be now opened for the performance of that ceremony. This my will and pleasure you will communicate to the Right Worshipful Junior Grand Warden, and he to the Brethren present, that all having due notice may govern themselves accordingly.

Senior Grand Warden.—Right Worshipful Junior Grand Warden: It is the order of the Most Worshipful Grand Master of the Grand Lodge of the State of Maryland, that this Corner-Stone be now laid with Masonic honors. This his will and pleasure you will proclaim to all present, that the occasion may be observed with due order and solemnity.

Junior Grand Warden.—Brethren, and all who are present, take notice, that the Most Worshipful Grand Master will now proceed to lay this Corner-Stone of the Monument in due Masonic form. You will observe the order and decorum becoming the solemn and important ceremonies in which we are about to engage.

HYMN.—*Tune "America."*

Father of love and might,
Send forth thy holy light
   On us to shine;
Be thou our Sovereign Lord,
And May thy Holy Word
Be to us shield and sword,
   Master Divine.

Bound in one Brotherhood,
Owning one common blood,
   Children of thine;
Fill us with kindliness,
Prompt to relieve distress,
Wearing thy true impress,
   Master Divine.

> With joyful hands, to-day,
> This Corner-Stone we lay
>   With Corn and Wine;
> But do thou build up one,
> Wrought in the living stone
> Of our true hearts alone,
>   Master Divine.
>
> Saviour Omnipotent,
> Crown Thou our good intent,
>   With grace of Thine:
> Honor this stone we rear;
> And when thou shalt appear,
> Save us who gather here,
>   Master Divine.

PRAYER, ... BY THE GRAND CHAPLAIN.

Grand Master.—Right Worshipful Grand Treasurer: You will read the inscription on the Corner-Stone, and list of the contents of the box.

(The Grand Treasurer will here read the contents.)

Grand Master.—There being no objection, I now order you, Brother Grand Treasurer, to deposit the Box, with its contents, in the place prepared for its reception.

The principal Architect then presents the Working Tools to the Grand Master, who directs the Grand Marshal to present them to the Deputy Grand Master, and Senior and Junior Grand Wardens.

SOLEMN MUSIC BY THE BAND.

The Grand Master, the Deputy Grand Master and Grand Wardens then descend from the platform, the Grand Master taking the Trowel, the Deputy Grand Master the Square, and the Senior Grand Warden the Level, and the Junior Grand Warden the Plumb; the Grand Master standing at the *East* of the Stone, his Deputy on his right, the Senior Grand Warden at the *West*, and the Junior Grand Warden at the *South* side of the Stone. The Grand Master then spreads the cement; after which he directs the Grand Marshal to order the Craftsmen to lower the Stone. [This is done by three motions, viz:—1st, by lowering a few inches and stopping, when *public* Grand Honors are given; 2d, again lowering a few inches, and giving Grand Honors; 3d, letting the Stone down to its place and giving Grand Honors as before. The Square, Level and Plumb are then applied to the Stone by the proper Officers.]

Grand Master.—Right Worshipful Deputy Grand Master: What is the proper Jewel of your office?

Deputy Grand Master.—The Square.

Grand Master.—Have you applied the Square to those parts of the Stone that should be square?

Deputy Grand Master.—I have, Most Worshipful Grand Master, and the Craftsmen have done their duty.

Grand Master.—Right Worshipful Senior Grand Warden: What is the proper Jewel of your office?

Senior Grand Warden.—The Level.

Grand Master.—Have you applied the Level to the Stone?

Senior Grand Warden.—I have, Most Worshipful Grand Master, and the Craftsmen have done their duty.

Grand Master.—Right Worshipful Junior Grand Warden: What is the proper Jewel of your office?

Junior Grand Warden.—The Plumb.

Grand Master.—Have you applied the Plumb to the several edges of the Stone.

Junior Grand Warden.—I have, Most Worshipful Grand Master, and the Craftsmen have done their duty.

Grand Master.—This Stone having been duly tested and found to be well-formed, true and trusty, it remains for me to finish the work.

The Grand Master then gives three knocks upon the Stone, saying—

"Men and Brethren here assembled, be it known unto you, that we are free and lawful Masons, true and faithful to the laws of our country, professing to fear God, and confer benefits on mankind. We have amongst us concealed from the eyes of man secrets which cannot be divulged, and which have never been discovered by the outside world; but those secrets are lawful and honorable, and not repugnant to the laws of God or man. Unless our Craft were good and our calling honorable, we should not have lasted for so many centuries, nor should we have been honored with the patronage of so many illustrious men in all ages, who have ever shown themselves ready to promote our interests and defend us from our adversaries. We have assembled here, to-day, in the face of this vast company, to lay the Corner-Stone of this Monument, which we trust may be safely completed and stand for ages both as an ornament to this place and a Monument to the ashes of the thousands who repose around it." So mote it be.—Amen.

ANTHEM, ... BY THE CHOIR.

The Grand Marshal then presents to the Deputy Grand Master the Cornucopia containing Corn, which he pours upon the Stone.

The Grand Marshal then presents the Cup of Wine to the Senior Grand Warden, who pours it on the Stone.

The Grand Marshal then presents the Cup of Oil to the Junior Grand Warden, who pours it on the Stone.

Grand Master.—May the All-Bounteous Author of Nature bless the inhabitants of this country with all the necessary conveniences and comforts of life, assist in the erection and completion of this Monument, protect the workmen against every accident, and long preserve this structure from decay—so that it may stand in all its beauty long after the bodies of those deposited here shall have crumbled into sepulchral dust; and finally grant us all a supply of the Corn of Nourishment, the Wine of Refreshment, and the Oil of Joy. So mote it be.—Amen.

The Grand Master then delivers over the various implements of architecture to the principal Architect, saying :

WORTHY SIR.—Having thus, as Grand Master of Masons of the State of Maryland, laid the Corner-Stone of this structure, I now deliver these implements of your profession into your hands, intrusting you with the superintendence and direction of the work, having full confidence in your skill and capacity to conduct the same.

CONCLUDING ODE.

MUSIC—"TURIN."

Placed in form the Corner-Stone,
True and Trusty, Brothers own,
Come and bring in thought sincere,
Hands to help, and hearts to cheer.
Chorus.—Come and bring, &c.

Marked with love, the Master's will
Kindly proved the work of skill—
Beauteous forms in grace shall rise
'Neath the arch of favoring skies.
Chorus.—Beauteous forms, &c.

Join we now our offering true
While our homage we renew;
Bear to Him whose praise we sing
Thanks that from each bosom spring.
Chorus.—Bear to him, &c.

When on Earth our work is o'er,
Be a dearer life in store,
Each in form, in heart upright,
Taught by truth's unerring light.
Chorus.—Each in form, &c.

BENEDICTION, . BY THE GRAND CHAPLAIN.

MUSIC.

EXTRACTS FROM THE ORATION OF EX-GOVERNOR BRADFORD AT THE DEDICATION OF ANTIETAM NATIONAL CEMETERY, SEPTEMBER 17TH, 1867.

We have met here to-day, my countrymen, on one of the most memorable of the battlefields of our civil war, and we stand upon a site selected from the midst of it as an appropriate resting place for those who here laid down their lives as a sacrifice to the cause of free government and a National Union. We have come at the instance of the Trustees, to whom the subject has been more especially committed, to dedicate by some public and official proceeding, on this, the anniversary of the battle, the spot so selected, hallowed as it is already with every hill around it, in the heart of the nation.

To unite in this ceremony, the President of the United States, several members of the Cabinet, the Chief Justice of the United States, members of the National Legislature, Governors, or other distinguished representatives of most of the States whose citizens formed the Army of the Union, have honored us with their presence, meaning, I am sure, for themselves and those they represent, to express by that presence their enduring gratitude to the soldiers, living or dead, who so nobly stood by them in their darkest hour of trial.

When, directly after the battle of Antietam, an order was issued by the Executive of Maryland returning thanks to the officers and men of the Union army who had so successfully expelled the invader from our State, the Commanding General of that army, to whom it was transmitted, responded to it in terms that challenged our attention. Expressing, on behalf of the Army of the Potomac, their thanks for our appreciation of their achievements, and their hopes that no Rebel army would again pollute our State, he concluded by committing to us e remains of their gallant comrades who now rest beneath its soil. A commission so touchingly confided to the people of the State, to say nothing of the duty otherwise incumbent on them, could never become with them a subject of indifference or neglect, and at the first meeting therefore of their representatives in the General Assembly of January, 1864, an act was passed authorizing the purchase of a part of the battlefield for the reception of its dead, and an appropriation of five thousand dollars placed at the command of the Governor for that purpose. Directly thereafter he visited the ground, examined it, and after consultation with prominent citizens, selected this spot, embracing in its view the most interesting points to the field of battle, as the proper site for the cemetery to become, in time, a place worthy the noble purpose to which we to-day devote it, and of the nation to whom the charge of it should properly belong.

In reviewing the details of the sanguinary conflict to which we are about to refer, we find some difficulty, with all the assistance that established peace and the lapse of time have furnished, to fix with proper historical accuracy some of the facts immediately connected with it. The Union Army comprised 87,164 men of all arms, the Confederate force upwards of 97,000 men.

The battle of the 17th opened at the dawn of day on the spot where the skirmish of the previous evening had closed; each side seemed to have looked to this point as the one to be particularly strengthened, and as though anticipating the tremendous struggle of which it was to be the centre. General Mansfield's corps, composed of the two divisions of Generals Green and Williams, had crossed over in the night and taken post a mile to the rear of General Hooker; whilst on the Confederate side General Jackson had brought one of his divisions to the front, and substituting two of his brigades for those of Hood, that had suffered from the engagement the previous evening, placed the other—the old Stonewall division—in reserve in the woods on the west side of the Hagerstown road.

In the whole history of the battlefields of the rebellion, it would be perhaps difficult to find a spot which for an entire day was assailed and defended with such persevering, obstinate and concentrated valor as the one to which I now refer, embracing the ground on both sides of the road, just mentioned and in close proximity to yonder little church that nestles now so quietly in the margin of the woods.

On the extreme left of our line the Ninth Army Corps, under General Burnside, occupied, during the forenoon, the left bank of the Antietam, near the lower bridge, waiting a favorable opportunity for forcing a passage. The precipitous character of the banks of the creek at that point, and the advantageous position secured by the enemy's batteries along these heights to the west of it, postponed, it would seem, that opportunity until about one o'clock; but at that hour a gallant charge of the 51st New York and 51st Pennsylvania Regiments carried the bridge, and crossing by that and a neighboring ford the whole Corps crossed over. The bridge has been known in the neighborhood ever since the battle as the Burnside Bridge, which name for its pastoral as well as patriotic significance it will probably retain forever.

Thus ended only, for want of light to pursue it further, a battle that had raged for nearly fourteen hours, and which beyond doubt was the fiercest and bloodiest of the war.

Twelve thousand of our dead and wounded warriors, and at least as many more of the enemy lay stretched upon the field.

Thus in our heart would we enshrine the memory of the Union soldiers; generations yet unborn shall recount to their offspring the history of their valor; and long after brass and marble have crumbled into dust, shall their names be preserved as the men who perished to perpetuate what their fathers had so struggled to establish—this Heaven-appointed Government of popular freedom.

ANTIETAM NATIONAL CEMETERY.

The following hymn was then sung:

HYMN II—"*America.*"

Hallowed be all around!
This place is holy ground,
   Henceforth, for aye;
Here mountain shadows wave
O'er many a cherished grave,
Where sleep the young and brave,
   Home from the fray!

Here where the flash and roar
Battle and carnage bore
   Over the main,
Soft, on your lowly bed
Rest your fame-laurel'd head
Our noble patriot dead
   By treason slain!

Grief stricken hearts have throbbed—
Sable clad homes have sobbed
   Far from your rest;
Listen for steps in vain,
That ne'er shall come again,
To swell the victor's train
   From East to West!

Antietam's liquid gem
Murmurs your requiem
   In mournful strain!
Angels unseen stand near,
Bright guard of honor here.
Till Christ, our Lord appear,
   Mighty to reign!

Silence and sadness round
No bugle's martial sound
   Your sleep breaks now.
Columbia, saved, now sheathes
Her conquering sword; Fame wreathes
Where'er true manhood breathes,
   Your pale, cold brow!

"Glory to God on high,"
Peal through earth, sea and sky,
   "Good Will to Men!"
Blending and rising higher,
Like Pentecostal fire,
Let Freedom's strains inspire
   All hearts! *Amen!*

After the singing of the hymn, the poem written by Clarence F. Buhler, of New York, who was absent by reason of illness, was read by G. L. Cranmer, Esq., the Trustee of the State of West Virginia, as follows:

THE DEDICATION POEM.

Upon a bright September morn,
  Five years ago to-day,
The pleasant hills of Maryland
  Green and untrodden lay;
While autumn leaves were strewn around
  In purple and in gold,
Like that Assyrian host o'er which
  The plague at midnight rolled.

The pheasant beat his long tattoo
  Where soon the drum would play,
And merrily Antietam creek
  Went singing on its way;
But many a tattered banner thrilled
  Upon the armory wall,
As if it felt the coming
  Of a tempest soon to fall.

The tramp of Lee's battalions
  Struck faintly on the ear,
As thunder in the distance tells
  A storm is drawing near;
While stretched along yon bristling height
  The Rebel files of gray,
Like leaden clouds that soon would burst
  In ruin and dismay.

But round the flag of freedom
  Her stalwart yeomen stood,
Resolved its stars should never set
  Till they went down in blood.
No flower of speech lost on the blast
  Had answered her appeal,
But marches like a gathering storm,
  Or avalanche of steel.

With every hamlet adding
  To the thunder of their tread,
As if the Revolution's graves
  Were giving up their dead;
And students fighting in their dreams
  The Punic wars again,
Wake in a holier cause to bleed
  On red Antietam's plain.

The combat opened; and between
  The valleys whistling then,
From every sulphur cloud was heard,
  The cheers of Hooker's men;
And where the yellow corn had waved
  Artillery sowed the field,
With shot and shell that make it still
  An iron harvest yield.

'Mid showers of grape and cannister,
  Along our lines of blue,
The soul of seventy-six struck with
  The arm of sixty-two.
Beneath our flag, the Lord of Hosts
  Fought on this reeking sod,
For traitors to their country
  Are traitors to their God.

In freedom's holy brotherhood
  The Saxon and the Gaul,
Shoulder to shoulder as they fell,
  Shared glory's crimson fall.
The Pennsylvania husbandman
  And Western mountaineer
Across the swarthy raider lay
  With empty musket, here.

Here fell the dauntless Mansfield,
  Whose streaming locks of snow
Could never for a moment chill
  The fiery heart below;
And yonder bridge that Burnside
  So gallantly did hold,
Is now as classic as the past
  The Spartans held of old.

Young Rodman as he prostrate lay
  Still waved his flag on high,
And faintly with his dying breath
  Sent up a battle cry.

Well might Duryea, as true a knight
  As ever couched a lance,
Smile grimly to behold his Zouaves
  With springing step advance;
And in their onset Meagher's brigade
  Of Erin's hardy sons
Paused not till they were looking down
  The muzzles of the guns.

The hardy form of Hooker
  Tossed on the surging flood,
'Till he had shown a rifleman
  The color of his blood;
While Sumner, Meade and Sedgwick,
  Like old campaigners, made
Raw striplings breast like regulars
  The gallant cannonade.

Historic Maryland! Such deeds
  Have made, with brilliant gleam,
A Marathon of every plain,
  A Nile of every stream;

DEDICATION POEM.

And nevermore would Europe boast
  Of her scarred grenadiers,
Could she have seen the work that day
  By our volunteers.

Four times yon wood was won and lost,
  Where lay the foe entrenched,
And to its staff our banners clung
  In scarlet rain bedrenched;
When onward swept the brawny troops
  That never charged in vain,
Our lion-souled Green Mountain boys
  And lumbermen of Maine.

And from their masked entrenchments
  The veteran ranks within
Were hurled as if each bayonet
  A thunderbolt had been.

Ah! sweetly by the planter's porch
  The orange tree will rise,
But never more its snowy bloom
  Will cheer his wistful eyes.
For many a year to come his blood,
  That blade or bullet drew,
Will make thy roses, Maryland,
  Spring with a redder hue.

Thin grew the host that fought beneath
  The fallen stars, and then,
Like gray wolves, backward, inch by inch,
  Retreating to their den.
Unto the cover of their works
  The baffled horde withdrew,
And soon upon the dust of strife
  The evening sprinkled dew.

Then martial strains rose from our camp,
  And as the wounded listened,
The nerveless hand was clenched again—
  Again the glazed eye glistened;
Some thought of fair ones, who afar
  Would name them from the pillow,
Or maidens who that night would sit
  Alone beneath the willow.

Some thought of stately marble halls,
  That in the city tower'd,
And others of a humble cot,
  Amid the vines embower'd;
Yet, whereso'er their thoughts were turned,
  As memory's magnet drew them,
The spot was hallowed by the name
  Of "Home, Sweet Home," unto them.

But when the morn in beauty broke,
Those heroes who had striven
So nobly for their homes, had found
A better home in heaven.
Then, softer grew the hard brown hand,
As with a woman's care,
Rough soldiers gently bore away
Their fallen comrades there.

And when the last long trench had closed
Above unnumbered slain,
All grades forgot an army lay
Encamped beneath this plain!
Yes! in dark barracks underneath
Rest those who chose the cypress wreath,
In service brief as glorious gained,
To laurels with dishonor stained.

Rest, till with those who bivouac still
At Marathon and Bunker Hill,
By louder trump than battle drew,
They've marshalled for the last review.
No more the pulse that beats so true
Will quicken as the loud tattoo
Ascends at sunrise from the camp,
Or sternly beat the measured tramp:

But hands unseen will hither bring
The earliest violets of the spring;
And pilgrims who have viewed with awe
The ruins of that haunted shore,
Where shrouds of lava overspread
The silent cities of the dead,
And every step brings through the gloom
An echo from storied tomb—
No longer o'er the deep will roam,
To leave a holier shrine at home!
For every clod we tread to-day
Is moulded from some hero's clay.
And looking downward from the skies,
Perchance the melancholy eyes
Of Lincoln wear a tender glow
As on this scene he gazes now.
I feel a God-like presence near—
The Great Emancipator's here!
O death! where is thy sting? O grave!
Where is thy victory o'er the brave?
Not with dim sight and tottering frame,
They sought the dust from which they came,
With eye whose flash seemed of the storm,
And war embodied in each form,
They marched at Glory's clarion call
To graves as to a banquet hall;
And though sweet voices filled each wind
Frome home, cast not one look behind,
Through such heroic souls as those
The Lord of Hosts his God-head shows!

DEDICATION POEM.

Over them no mournful requiem floats,
But bugles peal their loudest notes,
As to the heaven of Fame they march
Beneath our flag—its rainbow arch,
With an eternal furlough blest,
Sweet, sweet shall be the patriot's rest.
Fatigued with toil whose fruits sublime
Are building on the bough of Time,
And while above these sainted brave
One stripe of their old flag shall wave,
This consecrated spot will be
A sacred Mecca of the free.

HOSPITAL SCENE.

Speech of President Johnson.

MY FELLOW COUNTRYMEN: In appearing before you, it is not for the purpose of making any lengthy remarks, but simply to express my approbation of the ceremonies which have taken place to-day. My appearance on this occasion will be the speech that I will make. My reflections and my meditations will be in direct communion with the dead whose deeds we are here to commemorate.

I shall not attempt to give utterance to the feelings of emotion inspired by the addresses and prayers which have been made, and the hymns which have been sung. I shall attempt no such thing. I am merely here to give my countenance and aid to the ceremonies on this occasion; but I may be permitted to express the hope that we may follow the example which has been so eloquently alluded to this afternoon, and which has been so clearly set by the illustrious dead. When we look on yon battlefield, I think of the brave men who fell in the fierce struggle of battle, and who sleep silent in their graves. Yes, many of them sleep in silence and peace within this beautiful inclosure after the earnest conflict has ceased. Would to God, we of the living could imitate their example, as they lay sleeping in their tombs, and live together in friendship and peace. [Applause.]

You, my fellow citizens, have my earnest wishes as you have had my efforts in time gone by, in the earliest and most trying perils, to preserve the Union of these States, to restore peace and harmony to one distracted and divided country; and you shall have my efforts in vindication of the flag of the Republic, and of the Constitution of our forefathers.

The benediction was then pronounced, when the President, Cabinet officers, Governor Swann, and others, left the platform.

Colonel J. M. Moore and his assistants formed the military, who escorted the President and party to the cars at Keedysville, which place they left at ten minutes to seven o'clock for Washington and Baltimore.

Calls were renewed for Governor Geary by the crowd, which constituted a meeting independent of the regular arrangements by the authorities of the State and the Board of Managers of the Antietam National Cemetery.

Governor Geary, being emphatically and vociferously called for, came forward, saying:

FELLOW CITIZENS: After all you have heard to-day I had supposed you would want nothing more. The programme opened and concluded with prayer. Those who have waited must come in at the close; but, my friends, we still have a place in the hearts of the people. [Applause.] When you come to Pennsylvania we will let everybody speak we want to hear. Thanks to Almighty God for his preservation and care of the country, we have no gag. [Applause].

We have no programme for this purpose. [Renewed applause.] We have no gag on our programmes; but I am not here to say anything on that subject. The orator of the day has presented to you the history of the great battle, which we are now seeking to commemorate in the dedication of this cemetery and the location of the monument in honor of the heroic dead, who, in the language of the lamented Lincoln, [Applause] died that the Government of the people, established by and for the people, should not perish from the earth. [Applause.] The battle of Antietam was fought under circumstances of the greatest depression, when public confidence was lost, and the Army of the Potomac had been greatly diminished by the disastrous campaign on the Peninsula and in Eastern Virginia, and the loss of twelve thousand men by the shameful surrender at Harper's Ferry. [Applause] In Lee's coming to fight the battle of Antietam he had therefore the prestige of his victories to begin with. [A voice—That's so.] To appreciate the victory here we must renew events by the most liberal logic known to military ethics. While the Army of the Potomac had lost more men than the Rebels according to the authority of the latter, Lee was obliged to flee from the field, acknowledged himself vanquished, and a true and hearty victory resulted to the Union army.

My fellow-citizens, I don't intend to detain you long here, [Cries of "Go on"] I feel it improper for me to let the occasion go past without placing on record the hundred regiments of Pennsylvania who fought here. [Cries of "Hurrah for Pennsylvania," "Go on".] I proudly place on record these regiments of my native State, and draw for her a full share of the Victory of Antietam. [Cheers.]

The Governor then recapitulated the numbers of the various Pennsylvania regiments, remarking by way of summary : Five regiments of cavalry, six battalions of artillery, and fifty regiments of infantry from the Keystone State in the battle of Antietam. From the records I have drawn the facts. I find them replete with the splendid achievements of these men, and while I earnestly claim for Pennsylvania all the honor she has won, I say it was here, as always with that great State when she presented her full strength of numbers, she carried the Government to a glorious victory. I would not detract in the least degree from the glory and honor of other States. I would not deprive them of one particle of the glory of their troops on this battlefield. It was one sacred flow of blood in crimson stain at Antietam, not to any particular troops. The Soldiers of the Country won this victory, and we are indebted to Maine, New York, Ohio, Maryland, Wisconsin, Iowa, Pennsylvania and other States for the victory, and whose sons perished on the field. They are as dear to us, and are cherished as kindly as our own. The sons of all dyed this soil with their blood, and when the day dawned on the battlefield, it found Union dead all commingled on the field of strife ; and while the sun continues to rise and set, and the dews distil from heaven, our children and our children's children will come hither to worship at this shrine, and they will recur to the patriotic dead here, and to the memory of those who fought and bled to preserve the Union and the rights of men, the rights of freemen in a preserved Republic. [Applause.] I have been speaking repeatedly for the last two or three days and will, therefore, conclude my remarks. There are here Governor Fenton, Lieutenant General Cox, and the Governor of Maine, whom, I have no doubt, you will be glad to hear. [Cries of "Go On,"] but Governor Geary withdrew after introducing Governor Fenton, of New York, who spoke as follows:

FELLOW CITIZENS:—I dislike to detain you even one minute, but hesitate to leave this place without saying a few words. It is not easy to find words to fully and fitly express my feelings, or that may be most appropriately employed in the name of my State, whose eight hundred sons here sleep. There are times when human speech is too poor and weak to embody the emotions which the recollections of heroic deeds inspire. New York had almost 27,000 men on this field of strife, and about one-eighth of them were killed and wounded, but New York was not alone here, nor were the mutilated and dead alone from her ranks. Others came to-day, as I come, the representatives of States, united and living through the sacrifices of their fallen also—whom the nation alike mourns—and with fitting ceremony indicate the place where the devotion and valor inspired of our christian civilization blazed in the red line around these hills, to go out no more while the page of history shall endure. The token of our gratitude which we propose to place over the dust which is henceforth sacred as the index that in fit eloquence of silence shall challenge the progress of mankind. The noblest thought of man, as to human rights; the utmost self-denial at the call of duty; the grandest example of national devotion of the strong to the weak, the characteristic of our great war here gaining firmer root, strengthened the trunk and extended the branches of the tree of freedom and peace, whose ripened fruit stands waiting for hands clear of all unfaithfulness and injustice. The oppressed of all lands, toiling and waiting for their harvest of freedom will evermore turn their faces toward our heroic struggle, and grow patient and strong. The statesman grappling the problems which impeded the progress of the people, baffled by selfishness, appalled by crime, or disheartend by indifference, looking to these heights above the clouds that surround him, shall see this pledge to liberty, and work on, and if it shall be at any time that wicked men seek to destroy or disturb human progress, reckoning on the ignorance which suffers, or the prejudice which bears the lowest and most friendless, will not they at least, pause before the upraised hand of our enfranchised people? True, we are not free from national trials; but, faithful still to liberty and justice, the result is not doubtful. And our lives also, as the lives of the men whose deeds we now celebrate, will be as sacred as they are, giving to the progress and happiness of mankind.

ORDER OF PROCESSION
AT THE
CEREMONIES OF THE DEDICATION
OF THE
ANTIETAM NATIONAL CEMETERY,
AND THE
LAYING OF THE CORNER-STONE
OF THE
MONUMENT
SEPTEMBER 17th, 1867.

Aids.   Chief Marshal.   Aids.
Lt. Col. James M. Moore, U. S. A.
Artillery.
Infantry.
General Grant and Staff.
Major General McClellan and Staff.
Major General Burnside and Staff.
Ex Officers and Soldiers of the Army of the Potomac.
Officers and Soldiers of the Armies of the United States.
Officers of the Navy and Marine Corps of the United States.
THE PRESIDENT OF THE UNITED STATES.
The Cabinet Ministers.
The Diplomatic Corps.
Vice-Admiral Porter and Staff.
The Chief Justice and Associate Justices of the Supreme Court of the United States.
The President of the Day and the Orator.
The Chaplain, Poet and Chorister.
The Committee of Arrangements.
The Members of the U. S. Senate and House of Representatives.
The Governors of the Several States and Territories and their Staffs.
Board of Managers of the Antietam National Cemetery.
Mayors of Baltimore and Washington, and other Cities.
Independent Order of Odd Fellows.
Knights Templar.
Masonic Fraternity.

PROGRAMME OF ARRANGEMENT
And Order of Exercises for the Ceremonies of the Dedication of the
Antietam National Cemetery,
And the Laying of the Corner-Stone of the Monument, September 17, 1867.

The Marshal and Assistant Marshals will assemble at Keedysville, at 9 o'clock a. m.

The Military will form at Keedysville, at 10½ a. m., on the pike leading to Sharpsburg, west of the railroad.

The Masons and other civic bodies will form at the same time, on the pike leading to Sharpsburg, east of the railroad, with their right resting on the railroad crossing.

The head of the column will move at 11 o'clock a. m., up the pike to the Cemetery grounds.

The Military will form in line at the entrance to the Cemetery, (as may be directed,) and present arms when the President of the United States and all who are to occupy the stand shall pass to the same.

Ladies will occupy the left of the stand, and it is desirable that they be upon the ground as early as 11 o'clock a. m.

The Exercises will take place as soon as the entire procession is in position on the ground, as follows:

Music—Band.
Prayer by the Rev. Hiram Matison, D. D., of N. J.
Music—Band.
Introductory Remarks by the Governor of Maryland.
Music—Hymn, composed by Rev. Edward Meyer, of Pa., and sung by the Assemblage, under the Leadership of Wm. E. Macdonough, of N. Y.
Laying of the Corner-Stone by the Grand Master of the Grand Lodge of Masons of Maryland.
Music—Band.
Oration by Hon. A. W. Bradford, Ex-Governor of Maryland.
Music—Hymn, composed by Rev. Edward Meyer, of Pennsylvania.
Poem, by Clarence F. Buhler, of N. Y.
REMARKS BY THE PRESIDENT OF THE UNITED STATES.
Music—Band.
Benediction.
Music—Band.

After the Benediction, the procession will be dismissed, and the Marshal and Assistant Marshals will form and escort the President and party to the cars at Keedysville.

Salutes will be fired at sunrise, during the movement of the procession, and at the close of the exercises.

ASSISTANT MARSHALS.

Bt. Maj. Gen. Andrew W. Denison,
" " " E. B. Tyler,
" Brig. Chas. E. Phelps,
" " R. N. Bowerman,
" " Adam E. King,
" " H. R. Richardson,
" " John E. Mulford,

Bt. Maj. Gen. John R. Kenly,
Brig. Gen. J. W. Hoffman,
Col. John A. Tompkins,
" L. Blumenberg,
" Wm. H. Taylor,
" F. W. Simon,
Capt. Albert Grant.

JAMES M. MOORE, Chief Marshal.

ORATION OF ABRAHAM LINCOLN AT THE DEDICATION OF THE GETTYSBURG NATIONAL MILITARY CEMETERY, NOVEMBER 19TH, 1863.

Four score and seven years ago our fathers brought forth upon this continent a new nation, conceived in Liberty, and dedicated to the proposition that all men are created equal.

Now we are engaged in a great civil war, testing whether that nation, or any nation so conceived and so dedicated, can longer endure. We are met on a great battlefield of that war. We are met to dedicate a portion of it as the final resting place of those who here gave their lives that that nation might live. It is altogether fitting and proper that we should do this.

But in a larger sense we cannot dedicate, we cannot consecrate, we cannot hallow this ground. The brave men, living and dead, who struggled here have consecrated it far above our power to add or detract. The world will little note nor long remember what we say here, but it can never forget what they did here. It is for us, the living, rather to be dedicated here to the unfinished work that they have thus far so nobly carried on. It is rather for us to be here dedicated to the great task remaining before us—that from these honored dead we take increased devotion to the cause for which they here gave the last full measure of devotion—that we here highly resolve that the dead shall not have died in vain; that the nation shall, under God, have a new birth of freedom, and that the government of the people, by the people, and for the people, shall not perish from the earth.

CONNECTICUT.

Headst'e No.	NAME.	Rank.	Company	Regiment.	Arm of Service.	Date of Death.	REMARKS.
1085	Aldritch, Henry	Private,	K	16	Infantry,	Sept. 17, 1862	Killed in action.*
1196	Anderson, Wm. H.	"	M	1	Artillery,	Aug. 4, 1862	Age 23 years, from Bridgeport.
1116	Burr, Francis W.	"	G	16	Infantry,	Oct. 11, 1862	Died of wounds received Sept. 17, 1862.*
1117	Bently, John	"	F	8	"	Oct. 17, 1862	" " " " †
1127	Batty, Davis	"	H	11	"	Sept. 17, 1862	Killed in action, from Plainfield.*
1133	Beach, Benjamin J.	"	E	11	"	Sept. 17, 1862	" " " from Berlin.*
1137	Barnard, George M.	"	D	5	"	Nov. 21, 1862	Removed from Antietam.
1140	Bout, Daniel	"	D	16	"	Dec. 12, 1862	Killed in action, from Suffield.*
1191	Balcom, Anson F.	"	C	2	Heavy Art'y,	Oct. 12, 1864	Age 33, from Farrington.*
1090	Case, Oliver C.	"	B	8	Infantry,	Sept. 17, 1862	Killed in action.*
1105	Cowan, William	"	E	16	"	Oct. 22, 1862	Died of wounds received at Antietam.*
1110	Culver, Frederick D.	"	K	11	"	Oct. 26, 1862	" " " " "
1118	Case, Orville J.	"	A	16	"	Oct. 22, 1862	Died of disease near Antietam.*
1125	Carl, Martin	"	H	8	Cavalry,		Removed from Weverton.
1126	Castle, Morton	"	C	8	Infantry,	Oct. 17, 1862	Age 19.†
1138	Cunningham, John	"	K	14	"	Dec. 3, 1862	From Hartford.||
1141	Curtis, Hanford	"	A	14	"	Dec. 17, 1862	From Stratford.||
1095	Dagle, George V.	"	K	8	"	Sept. 17, 1862	Killed in battle Antietam.*
1107	Dodge, Henry C.	"	H	11	"	Nov. 16, 1862	Died from wounds received at Antietam.*
1192	Davis, Randolph	"	L	1	Cavalry,	Jan. 14, 1865	From Meriden.||
1188	Dooling, Jas.	"	D	16	"	July 8, 1862	Removed from Frederick.
1084	Evans, Henry D.	"	—	1	"	Sept. 17, 1862	Killed in action at Antietam.*
1139	Evans, Leverett F.	-	A	16	"	Nov. 15, 1862	From Bradford.||
1094	Finken, Henry	"	K	8	Infantry,	Sept. 17, 1862	Killed in action Antietam.*
1097	Fessington, Clinton	"	E	11	"	Sept. 21, 1862	Died of wounds received at Antietam.*
1101	Foster, Philip H.	"	B	16	"	Sept. 17, 1862	Killed in battle Antietam.*
1106	Fanning, Henry C.	"	D	8	"	Oct. 28, 1862	Died of wounds Antietam.*
1112	Farmer, W.	Corporal,	D	8	"		Removed from Antietam.
1120	Ford, John	Private,	—	1	Cavalry,	Oct. 17, 1864	Died at Harpers Ferry, gun shot wounds.*
1082	Greegin, James	"	—	16	Infantry,	Sept. 17, 1862	Killed in action.*
1088	Gladding, Timothy	"	G	16	"	Sept. 17, 1862	" " " *

DESCRIPTIVE LIST.

No.	Name	Rank	Co.	Regt.	Date	Remarks
1093	Grosvenor, Joseph A.	Private,	B	16 Infantry,	Sept. 17, 1862	Killed in action.*
1081	Hinnes, Stephen	"	L	" "	Sept. 17, 1862	Killed in battle Antietam.*
1091	Hinnes, James	"	B	" "	Sept. 25, 1862	Died of wounds Antietam.*
1092	Hamilton, Hancey	"	L	" "	Sept. 17, 1862	Killed Antietam.*
1098	Hull, Richard L.	Corporal,	H	14 " "	Sept. 25, 1862	Killed Antietam.*
1104	Hollister, Bridgman J.	Private,	B	16 " "	Oct. 12, 1862	Died of wounds Antietam.*
1113	Hunn, Horace	"		2 " "	Dec. 1, 1862	Died Big Spring Hospital.‖
1190	Hooker, Frederick	"	L	5 Heavy Art'ry,	Aug. 23, 1864	Age 19, from Fartington‖
1187	Hills, Percival S.	"	B	5 Infantry,	June 24, 1862	Age 40, from Bristol.‖
1184	Hopper, Joseph	"		" "	Jan. 20, 1862	From Salisbury.‖
1183	Haverty, Daniel	"	H	" "		1862	From Manchester.*
1087	Kent, John S.	"	G	16 " "	Sept. 17, 1862	Killed in battle Antietam,*
1111	Kimball, Andrew J.	"	F	8 " "	Nov. 19, 1862	Wounded Sept. 17, 1862, died of disease at Keedysville, Md.
1099	Loveland, John	"	C	16 " "	Sept. 18, 1862	Removed from Antietam.
1100	Lay, Horace	"	L	16 " "	Sept. 17, 1862	Died of wounds received at Antietam.†
1123	Logan, George E.	"	L	8 " "	Nov. 15, 1862	" " ‡
1182	Lane, Horace F. L.	"	B	5 " "	Feb. 23, 1862	Died of disease, Weverton, Md.§
1181	Leggett, Elijah	"	E	5 " "	Feb. 14, 1862	From Bristol.*
1080	McGrath, James	"	E	16 " "	Sept. 17, 1862	Killed in action Antietam.*
1107	Morgan, Robert P.	"	E	16 " "			Died of wounds received at Antietam.‡
1121	Molloy, William	"	L	2 Cavalry,			
1134	Porter, James M.	"	A	4 Infantry,	Sept. 6, 1861	Removed from Hagerstown.*
1114	Remington, Thomas F.	"	K	11 " "	Sept. 26, 1862	Died of wounds received September 17, 1862.‖
1193	Robinson, Joseph	"	E	2 Artillery,	Sept. 17, 1861	From Norfolk, Connecticut.*
1177	Rising, Henry	"	D	11 Infantry,	Sept. 17, 1862	From Mathersfield, Connecticut.*
1176	Rodgers, Samuel C.	"	H	11 " "	Sept. 17, 1862	From Ledyard, Conn.*
1086	Smith, Michael	"	G	16 " "	Sept. 17, 1862	Killed in battle Antietam.*
1109	Schofield, Henry M.	"	H	11 " "	Sept. 28, 1862	Died of wounds received September 17, 1862.*
1115	Strickland, Henry E.	"	C	8 " "	Oct. 17, 1862	Died of wounds received September 17, 1862.*
1132	Schalk, John	"	C	18 " "	Aug. 16, 1863	Removed from Hagerstown.†
1142	Stannard, Ezra D.	"	G	14 " "	Dec. 21, 1862	Age 21, from Westbrook, Connecticut.‖
1194	Slade, Frederick	"	L	2 Artillery,	Sept. 24, 1864	From Bridgeport, Connecticut.‖
1186	Stevens, Henry S.	"	F	12 Infantry,	Aug. 17, 1864	Age 39, from Madison, Connecticut.*
1189	Stevens, Henry	"	E	4 " "	Sept. 17, 1861	From Chesline, Connecticut.*
1083	Twiss, Jason, E.	"	I	16 " "	Sept. 17, 1862	Killed in battle of Antietam.°
1179	Tarbox, George W.	"	E	18 " "	Aug. 10, 1864	From Columbia, Connecticut.

*Removed from Antietam. †Rem'd from Hagerstown. ‡Rem'd from Weverton. §Rem'd from Frederick. ‖Rem'd from Hancock. °Rem'd from Clarysville.

CONNECTICUT—Continued.

Head'stone No.	NAME.	Rank.	Company.	Regiment.	Arm of Service.	Date of Death.	REMARKS.
1178	Taylor, Jarvis	Private,		16	Infantry,	Oct. 23, 1862	Removed from Hancock.
1096	Unknown—Connecticut,	"			"		Removed from Antietam.
1119	" "	"		20	"		" "
1128	" "	"		20	"		" " Hagerstown.
1129	" "	"		20	"		" "
1130	" "	"			"		
1180	Vananken, Frank	"	G	5	"	Feb. 1, 1862	From Stonington, Conn., rem'd f'm Hancock.
1089	Wilsey, Julius C.	"	H	16	"	Sept. 17, 1862	Killed in battle Antietam.*
1103	Wilson, Frederick	"	D	8	"	" "	" " "
1108	Wilson, Orvil M.	"	G	16	"	Nov. 2, 1862	Died of wounds received at Antietam.‡
1124	White, John J.	"	A	16	"	Feb. 13, 1863	Died from chronic diarrhea.
1131	Welton, Harvey S.	"	C	27	"	July 14, 1862	Age 19, removed from Hagerstown.
1135	Webster, John R.	"	K	14	"	Oct. 6, 1862	Removed from Frederick.
1136	Wardwell, Emerson	"	D	16	"	Oct. 17, 1862	From Enfield, Connecticut.‖
1197	Weed, Raymond	"	B	17	"	July 7, 1862	Age 20, from Darien, Connecticut.
1195	Williams, W. M.	Sergeant,	E	11	"	Sept. 21, 1864	Removed from Frederick.
1185	Wheeler, Nathan S.	Private,	E	5	"	Aug. 28, 1861	From Norwalk, Connecticut.‡
1122	Yemmons, Joseph	"		8	"	Nov. 10, 1862	Died of disease, Weverton, Md.

DELAWARE.

Head'stone No.	NAME.	Rank.	Company.	Regiment.	Arm of Service.	Date of Death.	REMARKS.
3059	Ardis, Richard	Private,	F	3	Infantry,	Dec. 20, 1862	Removed from Frederick, Md.
3049	Brinkman, Adolph	"	E	2	"	Sept. 17, 1862	Killed in action Antietam.
3058	Blades, Major G.	"	D	1	"	Oct. 28, 1862	Removed from Frederick, Md.
3065	Burnes, Thomas	"	B	1	"	Mar. 11, 1867	" " "
3053	Connelly, Stephen,	"	B	2	"	Sept. 17, 1862	Killed in action Antietam.
3052	Cummons, William	"	E	2	"	Sept. 17, 1862	" " "
3111	Coleman, Henry	"		2	"	Oct. 2, 1862	Removed from Frederick, Md.
3112	Duffee, D.	"	C	1	"	Oct. 3, 1862	" " "
3042	Gentholz, Gottleib	"	F	2	"	Oct. 21, 1862	Removed from Smoketown, Md.

DESCRIPTIVE LIST.

No.	Name	Rank	Co.	Regt.		Date		Remarks
3056	Gorman, William	Corporal,	I	3	Infantry,	Oct.	14, 1862	Removed from Frederick, Md.
3357	Gregory, Philip	Private,	H	1	"	Oct.	18, 1862	" " " "
3113	Isams, Charles	"	C	1	"	Oct.	3, 1862	" " " "
3064	Jones, S. S.	"	A	3	"	Mar.	1, 1863	" " " "
3045	Livsley, John	"	F	3	"	Sept.	17, 1862	Killed in action at Antietam, Md.
3060	Lofland, Joshua	"	H	3	"	Jan.	12, 1863	Removed from Frederick, Md.
3063	Lank, M.	"	C	3	"	Dec.	26, 1862	" " " "
3054	Mumford, Samuel	"	E	2	"	Oct.	18, 1862	Removed from Smoketown, Md.
3046	Orskins, Thomas	"	A	1	"	Sept.	17, 1862	Removed from Antietam.
3055	Porter, John	"	H	1	"	Oct.	16, 1862	Removed from Frederick, Md.
3110	Parson, Lander C.	"	B	3	"	Aug.	5, 1862	
3051	Quigley, Edward	"	L	2	"	Sept.	17, 1862	Killed in action Antietam.
3062	Russell, Benjamin S.	Corporal,	I	2	"	Jan.	3, 1863	Removed from Frederick, Md.
3050	Savoy, William P.	Private,	D	2	"	Sept.	17, 1862	Killed in action Antietam.
3047	Sheppard, Elie	"	A	1	"	Sept.	17, 1862	" " " "
3014	Spicer, Philip R.	Sergeant,	G	1	"	Sept.	20, 1862	" " " "
3043	Shronk, Joseph	Private,	B	2	"	Sept.	17, 1862	" " " "
3061	Seville, W. F.	"	G	1	"	Jan.	11, 1863	Removed from Frederick, Md.
3048	Tapper, George	"	E	2	"	Sept.	17, 1862	

ILLINOIS.

No.	Name	Rank	Co.	Regt.		Date		Remarks
3066	Bailey, R. S.	Private,	F	8	Cavalry,	July	10, 1863	Died of wounds at Frederick, Md., aged 21‖
3069	Baker John T.	Bugler,	K	8	"	July	9, 1864	Removed from Frederick, Md.
3076	Borchers, Hermanus	Private,	G	39	Infantry,	Feb.	14, 1862	Died of disease at Cumberland, Md†
3038	Cole, J. W.	"	F	8	Cavalry,	July	15, 1863	Removed from Boonesboro.
3075	Collins, George	"	G	39	Infantry,	July	14, 1862	Died of disease in Fulton Co., Pa.
3105	Corwin, Squires	"	K	23	"	Sept.	29, 1864	Removed from Clarysville, Md.
3040	Dusold, J. G.	"	D	8	Cavalry,	July	10, 1863	Removed from Boonesboro.
3074	Dunham, Hiram G.	"	G	39	I., antry,	Feb.	23, 1852	Died of disease at Cumberland, Md.†
3067	Gilbert, C. S.	"	C	8	Cavalry,	July	12, 1864	Died at Frederick, Md.‖
3068	Greenville, Charles	"	K	8	"	July	9, 1864	Killed in action Frederick, Md.‖
3073	Helm, Willis N.	"	G	39		Aug.	10, 1862	Died of disease at Cumberland, Md.
3107	Hartman, William H.			39				Removed from Cumberland, Md.
3104	Hulihan, John	"	K	23		Feb.	7, 1864	Died of wounds received at Westernport, Md.§
3041	Kennicott, Walter J.	"	F	8	Cavalry,	July	15, 1863	Removed from Fulton Co., Pa. ○Rem'd from Westernport

*Rem'd from Antietam. †Rem'd from Weverton. ‡Rem'd from Frederick. ‖Rem'd from Cumberland. ○Rem'd from Westernport

40   ANTIETAM NATIONAL CEMETERY.

ILLINOIS—Continued.

Headst'e No.	NAME.	Rank.	Company	Regiment	Arm of Service.	Date of Death.		REMARKS.
3108	Littleton, W. S.	Private,		39	Infantry,			Died at Cumberland, Md.†
3036	McArthur, Robert	"		8	Cavalry,			Removed from South Mountain.
3931	Martin, Austin	"	B	8	"	Oct. 15,	1862	Died at Frederick, Md.*
3071	McLaughlin, John	"	G	23	Infantry,	Dec. 15,	1864	Died of wounds received at Frederick, Md.*
3109	Mott, George H.	"	G	39	"			Died at Cumberland, Md.†
3034	Parish, William C.	"	C	39	"	Nov. 29,	1851	Died at Antietam, aged 34.†
3106	Perry, William H.	"		39	"	Feb. 25,	1862	Died at Cumberland, Md.†
3035	Robbins, H. P.	"		5	"			Died at Weverton, Md.
3070	Ross, R.	"	H	8	Cavalry,	July 9,	1864	Died at Frederick, Md.*
3077	Rowley, Charles	"	G	39	Drummer,	Feb. 20,	1862	Died at Cumberland, Md.†
3033	Smith, William E.	Corporal,	F	8	Cavalry,	July 9,	1863	Killed in action, Frederick, Md.*
3932	Slater, J.	Private,		8	"	Sept. 29,	1862	Died at Frederick, Md.*
3072	Scott, George M.	"	B	65	Infantry,	Sept. 5,	1862	Died at Frederick, Md.*
3037	Unknown—Illinois			8	Cavalry,			Removed from Boonesboro'.
3039	Vinson, Richard C.	Sergeant,	K	8	"	July 6,	1863	Removed from Boonesboro'.

INDIANA.

Headst'e No.	NAME.	Rank.	Company	Regiment	Arm of Service.	Date of Death.		REMARKS.
3477	Allman, George	Private,	F	19	Infantry,	Oct. 11,	1862	Removed from Smoketown.
3447	Anderson, John R.	"	C	19	"	Sept. 17,	1862	Removed from Antietam Battlefield.
3448	Anton, Levi	"		19	"	Sept. 17,	1862	Killed in action.
3451	Addleman, Joseph O.	"	B	17	Battery,	Sept. 17,	1862	Removed from Antietam.
3488	Alexander, William B.	"		14	Infantry,	Apr. 21,	1864	Removed from Hagerstown.
3434	Bryant, Robert	Sergeant,	C	14	"			Removed from Antietam Battlefield.
3479	Barnes, Hugh	Private,	H	14	"	Oct. 10,	1865	Removed from Smoketown.
3492	Barnes, Levi	"	R	14	"	Oct. 1,	1862	Removed from Frederick.
3495	Buchanan, Pleasant	"	B	3	Cavalry,	Nov. 11,	1862	" "
3420	Boner, George W.	"	C	14	Infantry,	May 13,	1863	" "
3409	Bussard, William H.	"	A	150	"	Apr. 15,	1865	" "
3388	Bias, Green	"	H	27	"	Jan. 15,	1862	" "

DESCRIPTIVE LIST.

No.	Name	Rank	Co.	Regt.	Arm	Date	Year	Remarks
3377	Blasdel, I. F.	Private,	G	15	Infantry,	June 20,	1865	Removed from Clarysville, Md.
3369	Brandyberry, Ezra	"	H	147	"	May 3,	1865	"
3370	Blodkamp, Henry	"	C	152	"	Apr. 22,	1865	"
3438	Carlow, Thomas W.	Corporal,	K	14	"	Sept. 17,	1862	Removed from Antietam battlefield.
3449	Clark, John W.	Private,	I	19	"	Sept. 17,	1862	"
3450	Chamberlin, Napoleon	"	B	19	"	Sept. 17,	1862	"
3462	Conrad, John	"		27	"			"
3463	Cantwell, A. L.	"	E	27	"			"
3474	Clark, ——	"		12	"			"
3489	Coon, Benjamin	"	L	150	"	Aug. 3,	1861	Removed from Hagerstown.
3411	Curtis, Thomas	"	L	1	"	Apr. 11,	1865	Removed from Frederick.
3402	Coleman, Charles	"	E	16	"	Sept. 24,	1862	"
3385	Cooper, J. A.	"	G	7	"	Sept. 29,	1862	Removed from Cumberland.
3380	Corn, Moses	"	E	19	"	Sept. 29,	1862	Removed from Antietam battlefield.
3480	Dusang, Samuel G. W.	"	K	27	"	Jan. 18,	1863	Removed from Frederick.
3428	Duffy, James	"	E	27	"	Jan. 18,	1863	"
3425	Deputy, Henry	"	E	27	"	Jan. 1,	1862	"
3391	Davenport, E. M.	"	C	14	"	Feb. 25,	1862	Removed from Cumberland.
3374	Daily, John	"	A	7	"			"
3371	Davis, Matthias	"		27	"	Apr. 15,	1865	Removed from Antietam battlefield.
3452	Deputy, William	"	A	146	"	Oct. 13,	1862	Removed from Clarysville.
3366	Denham, Joseph	"	K	27	"	Oct. 27,	1862	Removed from Antietam battlefield.
3494	Delahunt, Wm.	"	D	14	"	Jan. 20,	1862	Removed from Frederick.
3470	Emery, Jonas	"	K	27	"			Removed from Cumberland.
3393	Evans, Joseph	"	G	13	"			Removed from Antietam battlefield.
3376	Elliott, Baker	"	D	27	"			"
3458	Fiddler, Joseph	"	E	27	"	Oct. 6,	1862	Removed from Frederick.
3431	Fulp, Emanuel	"	H	27	"	Nov. 27,	1862	Removed from Antietam battlefield.
3362	French, David J.	"	M	152	5 Cavalry,	Mar. 27,	1865	Removed from Clarysville.
3368	Finch, James	"	I	27	Infantry,	Mar. 18,	1865	Removed from Antietam battlefield.
3453	Good, Robert	Corporal,	C	27	"			"
3454	Gardner, John	Private,	B	19	"	Oct. 12,	1862	Removed from Smoketown.
3476	Gray, Jeduthan	"	G	150	"	Mar. 31,	1865	Removed from Frederick.
3412	Goodwine, Wm.	"	K	152	"	Apr. 4,	1865	"
3406	Grayham, Seymour	"	F	27	"	Feb. 25,	1862	"
3398	Goings, George W.							

†Removed from Cumberland.   *Removed from Frederick.   *Removed from Weverton.

INDIANA—CONTINUED.

Head'st'e No.	NAME.	Rank.	Company	Regiment	Arm of Service.	Date of Death.	REMARKS.
3397	Garrison, Joseph	Private,	C	27	Infantry,	June 29, 1862	Removed from Frederick.
3436	Harsh, Andrew	"	K	14	"	Sept. 17, 1862	Removed from Antietam battlefield.
3443	Hadley, Isaac N.	"	L	12	"	Oct. 28, 1861	Age 20—removed from Antietam battlefield.
3460	Hensley, W. J.	"	G	27	"	Sept. 17, 1862	Removed from Antietam battlefield.
3486	Ham, John W.	Corporal,	L	11	"		Removed from Hagerstown.
3423	Hawkins, Joseph	Private,	E	27	"	Dec. 22, 1862	Removed from Frederick.
3400	Hann, John H.	"	G	7	"	Oct. 4, 1862	"
3399	Hanna, William A.	"	B	3	Cavalry,	Sept. 30, 1862	"
3382	Hurst, Amer	"	B	16	Infantry,	Dec. 29, 1861	"
4217	Hansell, John W.	"	A	27	"		Removed from Antietam battlefield,
3473	Jones, Joshua	"	E	19	"	Oct. 29, 1862	"
3430	Johnson, Henry H.	"	L	19	"	Nov. 15, 1862	Removed from Frederick.
3435	Kelso, R. N.	"	G	14	"	Sept. 17, 1862	Removed from Antietam battlefield,
3441	Kehner, Daniel S.	"	A	14	"	Sept. 17, 1862	Removed from Antietam battlefield,
3475	Kinkle, George H.	"	E	14	"	Oct. 4, 1862	Removed from Smoketown.
3418	Kennedy, W. O.	Corporal,	F	3	"	Aug. 15, 1863	Age 29—removed from Frederick,
3410	Kiger, Elias D.	Private,	H	150	"	Apr. 10, 1865	Removed from Frederick.
3390	Kane, George W.	"	G	27	"	Dec. 26, 1861	"
3387	Kirkman, Madison	"		16	"		"
3364	Kilgore, James A.	"	D	150	"	May 3, 1865	Removed from Clarysville.
3455	Layman, Martin	"	C	27	"		Removed from Antietam battlefield,
3467	Logan, Nathan	"	E	27	"		"
3468	Lemming, Samuel S.	"			Indep't Vols.		"
3471	Lowrey, Thomas	"	H	19	Infantry,	Oct. 17, 1862	"
3452	Lacy, Louis	"	D	19	"	Sept. 14, 1862	Removed from Middletown.
3483	Laymon, William	"	H	19	"	Oct. 11, 1862	"
3485	Lewis, Joseph	Sergeant,	E	3	Cavalry,		"
3433	Lonsdale, Thos.	Private,	C	14	Infantry,	Oct. 28, 1862	Removed from Frederick.
3394	Lester, John F.	"	G	27	"	Jan. 4, 1862	"
3459	McLaughlin, Robert			27	"		Removed from Antietam battlefield.
3427	McIvery, G.		K	14	"	Dec. 2, 1862	Removed from Frederick.

DESCRIPTIVE LIST.

No.	Name	Rank	Co.	Regiment	Date	Year	Remarks
3408	Monsun, C. L.	Private,	K	147 Infantry,	April 3,	1865	Removed from Frederick.
3403	Mullen, J. B.	"	G	13 "	Aug. 14,	1862	"
3392	McCoy, Jesse C.	"	A	27 "	Mar. 12,	1862	"
3378	McGowen, Michael	"	A	154 "	June 7,	1865	Removed from Cumberland.
3373	Melton, William H.	"	K	144 "	April 5,	1865	"
3440	Nearon, Jacob	"	A	14 "	Sept. 17,	1862	Removed from Antietam battlefield.
3424	Nugen, Jasper	"	C	27 "	July 17,	1863	Removed from Frederick.
3139	O'Bryen, Frank			14 "			Removed from Frederick.
3464	Peters, John R.	"		27 "			Removed from Antietam battlefield.
3472	Parker, Thomas H.	"	C	19 "	Oct. 20,	1862	"
3432	Peters, John	"	C	14 "	Nov. 16,	1862	Removed from Frederick.
3417	Perry, L.	"	H	11 "	Sept. 13,	1864	"
3365	Powers, Earl	"	K	152 "	April 1,	1865	Removed from Clarysville.
3401	Quinn, James	"	F	3 Cavalry,	Sept. 30,	1862	Removed from Frederick.
3372	Queen, Joseph	"	A	14 Infantry,			Removed from Cumberland.
3342	Richard, John	"	C	14 "	Sept. 17,	1862	Removed from Antietam battlefield,
3345	Rich, Henry C.	"	E	19 "	Sept. 17,	1862	"
3496	Rollins, Sylvester	Corporal,	H	14 "	Oct. 17,	1862	Removed from Frederick.
3491	Rollins, Sylvester	Private,	B	14 "	Oct. 24,	1852	"
3416	Rust, Andrew J.	"	B	150 "	April 10,	1865	"
3404	Rush, George	"	C	150 "	April 4,	1855	"
3361	Rinehart, Abraham	"	E	152 "	April 2,	1865	Removed from Clarysville.
3367	Rumple, Jacob	"	B	53 "	Mar. 21,	1865	"
3437	Scott, Henry	"	C	14 "	Sept. 17,	1862	Removed from Antietam battlefield.
3446	—— D. W. S.	"	D	19 "			"
3456	Smith, W. H.	"		27 "	Sept. 17,	1862	"
3457	Smith, Franklin	"	E	27 "			"
3178	Steward, David	"	H	3 Cavalry,	Dec. 5,	1862	Removed from Smoketown.
3484	Seever, S. W.	"	E	27 Infantry,			Removed from Middletown.
3490	Schardien, William	"	D		June 18,	1862	Removed from Williamsport.
3421	Slough, A.	"	L	19 "	Feb. 19,	1863	Age 19 years, removed from Frederick.
3119	Slider, Wesley	"	D	27 "	April 3,	1863	Age 20 years, "
3305	Sims, Beverly	"	K	144 "	April 13,	1865	Removed from Frederick.
3375	Seemen, Jacob B.	Sergeant,	E	156 "	June 7,	1865	" Clarysville
3352	Scribner, Elmore	Private,	G	152 "	April 21,	1865	Removed from Frederick.
3429	Shupe, William J.	"	D	14 "	Dec. 4,	1862	Frederick.
3389	Tatlock, R. M.	"	F	27 "	Jan. 15,	1862	Removed from Frederick.
3426	Turner, W. H. H.	"	A	27 "	Jan. 14,	1862	"

ANTIETAM NATIONAL CEMETERY.

INDIANA—Continued.

Headst'e No.	NAME.	Rank.	Company	Regim't	Arm of Service.	Date of Death.	REMARKS.
3396	Tinder, Nathan	Private,	D	27	Infantry,	Mar. 5, 1862	Removed from Frederick.
3395	Taylor, Clayton	"	C	14	"	June 2, 1862	"
3379	Thomas, James	"	G	29	"		Removed from Cumberland.
3356	Turner, Marcus B.	"	F	152	"	April 13, 1865	Removed from Clarysville.
3358	Taylor, John T.	"	—	147	"	June 1, 1865	"
3414	Ungen, Peter	"	G	150	"	April 20, 1865	Removed from Antietam battlefield.
3465	Unknown,	"	F	12	"		"
3466	"			16			Removed from Hagerstown.
3487	"			16			Removed from Frederick.
3386	"			16			"
3384	"			16			"
3383	"			16			"
3381	"			11			"
3355	Vanorsdall, William			27			Removed from Cumberland.
3461	Vaughn, Richard	Private,	F	146	"	July 18, 1865	Removed from Antietam battlefield.
3360	Worster, Charles W.	Corporal,	H	12	"	Dec. 7, 1861	Age 21, removed from Clarysville.
3444	Willman, Jehiel	Private,		7			Removed from Antietam battlefield.
3481	Wiseman, H. W.	"	B	3	"	Oct. 15, 1862	Removed from Frederick.
3493	Wellens, H. C.	"	C	27	"	Dec. 27, 1862	"
3422	White, Harvey G.	"	D	150	"	April 2, 1865	"
3415	Webb, Joseph	"	L	14	"		Removed from Cumberland.
3353	Ward, Benjamin	"	F	147	"	April 8, 1865	"
3354	Watson, James	"	H	144	"	April 2, 1865	Removed from Clarysville.
3357	Wright, Greenberry	"	D	144	"	July 2, 1865	"
3359	Woodford, Byron D.	"	C	152	"	Mar. 25, 1865	"
3363	Young, Sampson	"	F	144	"	Mar. 27, 1865	Removed from Frederick.
3413	Young, James S.	"	G	150	"	April 2, 1865	"
3407							

DESCRIPTIVE LIST.   45

IOWA.

3029	Ardray, M. F.	Private,	D	24	Infantry,	Jan. 28, 1865 Removed from Frederick.
3030	Bolton, Abraham	"	H	24	"	Aug. 21, 1864 Age 28 years—Removed from Weverton.

MAINE.

3177	Adams, Eben	Private,	C	5	Infantry,	Oct. 28, 1862 Removed from Antietam battlefield.
3148	Brewer, Anderson	"	K	20	"	Sept. 17, 1862 " " "
3161	Brine, William	"	B	10	"	Sept. 17, 1862 " " "
3165	Bradbury, Hugh M.	"	H	10	"	Nov. 6, 1862 Removed from Smoketown.
3183	Bartlett, Marcus C.	"	G	10	"	Dec. 1, 1862 Removed from Weverton.
3196	Bridges, John C.	"	G	10	"	Aug. 27, 1864 " " "
3199	Barnes, John	"	F	37	"	Oct. 30, 1862 Removed from Hagerstown.
3200	Brown, James F.	"		6	"	July 12, 1863 Removed from Antietam battlefield.
3201	Boynton, W. S.	"	F	21	"	July 17, 1863 Removed from Hagerstown.
3207	Bean, Franklin	"	G	5	"	Jan. 28, 1863 Age 20.—Removed from Frederick.
3125	Babcock, Charles C.	"	B	6	"	Aug. 21, 1865 Removed from Frederick.
3120	Brooks, William H.	"	B	30	Cavalry,	Sept. 19, 1862 " " "
3119	Brock, Freeman	"	D	1	"	Oct. 9, 1862 " " "
3117	Bean, Charles H.	"	D	10	Infantry,	June 2, 1862 " " "
3116	Barker, Albert E.	"	A	10	"	Oct. 25, 1862 Removed from Antietam battlefield.
3115	Bean, Oscar F.	"	D	20	"	Sept. 17, 1862 " " "
3155	Clark, George A.	"		10	"	Oct. 9, 1862 " " "
3169	Campbell, Henry	"	G	6	"	Oct. 24, 1862 Removed from Smoketown.
3180	Chamberlin, L. G.	"		16	"	
3189	Corbett, Charles P.	Sergeant,	C	5	Artillery,	July 20, 1865 Removed from Middletown.
3192	Chadbourn, Edward C.	Private,	F	7	Infantry,	July 14, 1862 Age 19.—Removed from Frederick.
3194	C——, John H.	"	B	6	Infantry,	Mar. 17, 1862 Removed from Frederick.
3126	Campbell, Adna H. R.	"	F	1	Cavalry,	Oct. 24, 1863 Removed from Smoketown.
3114	Cushman, Fairfield	"	C	6	Infantry,	Nov. 23, 1862 Removed from Frederick.
3185	Day, George F.	"	C	29	Infantry,	Feb. 1, 1864 " " "
3140	Drake, Francis E.	"	D	29	"	Sept. 17, 1865
3123	Damren, Charles M.	"	K	10	"	Sept. 17, 1862 Removed from Antietam battlefield.
3122	Dicky, Orrin					
3159	Eaton, James D.					

MAINE—CONTINUED.

Headst'e No.	NAME	Rank	Company	Regim't	Arm of Service	Date of Death	REMARKS
3141	Easty, George W.	Private,	D	10	Infantry,	Oct. 23, 1862	Removed from Frederick.
3164	Fuller, George J.	"	H	10	"	Sept. 17, 1862	Removed from Antietam battlefield.
3190	Fossett, Robert M.	"	C	16	"	Oct. 25, 1862	Removed from Smoketown.
3191	Fletcher, Oliver	"	–	5	"		"
3197	Finney, Ira J.	"	C	1	Veteran,	Aug. 21, 1862	Removed from Weverton.
3133	Fisher, Ezra R.	"	–	4	Infantry,	Nov. 27, 1862	Removed from Frederick.
3131	Foss, Nathan A.	"	G	4	Battery,	June 3, 1863	"
3187	Goodwin, Arthur	"	C	16	Infantry,	Oct. 27, 1862	Removed from Smoketown.
3137	Hayes, William M.	"	F	1	Cavalry,	Nov. 10, 1862	Removed from Frederick.
3193	Hussey, Geo. Jr.	"	G	16	Infantry,	Oct. 18, 1862	Removed from Smoketown.
3147	Ireland, Rinaldo	"	B	20	"	Oct. 21, 1862	Removed from Antietam battlefield.
3171	Johnson, James	"	C	7	"	Sept. 17, 1862	"
3174	Jordan, James F.	"	F	10	"	Sept. 18, 1862	"
3179	Jones, Waldo B.	"	I	20	"	Oct. 27, 1862	"
3132	Jacquith, James	"	E	19	"	Nov. 27, 1862	Removed from Frederick.
3150	Littlefield, Moses	"	–	20	"	Oct. 30, 1862	Removed from Antietam battlefield.
3151	Lawber, Frederick T.	"	K	5	Battery,	Oct. 30, 1862	"
3321	Littlefield, Charles H.	"	G	10	Infantry,	April 25, 1865	Removed from Frederick.
3118	Logan, J. M.	"	B	10	"	Aug. 2, 1862	"
3166	Mason, Vincent	"	C	10	"	Sept. 17, 1862	Removed from Antietam battlefield.
3156	McCarthy, John	"	C	7	"	Sept. 17, 1862	Main Vol., rem'd from Antietam battlefield.
3162	McGinty, John	"	–	16	"	Nov. 6, 1862	Removed from Antietam battlefield.
3170	McPheters, Warren A.	"	C	20	"	Oct. 29, 1862	Removed from Smoketown.
3181	Mitchell, Joseph	"	–	16	"	Nov. 7, 1862	Removed from Antietam battlefield.
3149	Newbert, Neville A.	"	G	10	"	Sept. 17, 1862	Removed from Smoketown.
3182	Oakes, Charles	"	L	1	Cavalry,	Nov. 18, 1862	Removed from Antietam battlefield.
3168	Pressey, Charles M.	"	E	1	"	Nov. 14, 1862	Removed from Frederick.
3206	Pinkins, Charles	"	B	6	Infantry,	July 19, 1863	Age 20—Removed from Frederick.
3138	Pratt, Oliver P.						
3134	Pickard, John E.						
3128	Phillips, Jonathan K.	Corporal,					

DESCRIPTIVE LIST.

No.	Name	Rank	Co.	Regt.	Arm	Date	Year	Remarks
3124	Perkins, Orrin W. B.	Private,	D	30	Infantry,	Sept. 8,	1864	Removed from Frederick.
3158	Reed, Asa	"	K	10	"	Sept. 17,	1862	Removed from Antietam battlefield.
3184	Richardson, O. F.	"	E	6	"	Oct. 16,	1862	Removed from Smoketown.
3188	Rafford, James C.	"	C	16	"	Oct. 27,	1862	"
3195	Radcliffe, James H.	"	G	30	"	Sept. 6,	1864	Removed from Weverton.
3186	Ring, C. H.	"	C	18	"	Nov. 30,	1862	Removed from Smoketown.
3154	Spear, William F.	"	F	20	"	Oct. 23,	1862	Removed from Antietam battlefield.
3167	Stanley, George	"	G	10	"	Sept. 17,	1862	"
3172	Stickney, William C.	"	G	7	"	Sept. 17,	1862	"
3173	Sholes, W. L.	"	C	15	"			"
3168	Spencer, Harrison	"	H	12	1 Rifles,	Sept. 12,	1864	Removed from Weverton.
3146	Shlaffly, Christian	Corporal,	F	1	1 Cavalry,	Oct. 20,	1862	Removed from Frederick.
3139	Stacy, John S.	Private,	K	1	"	Nov. 9,	1862	"
3136	Shaw, William B.	"	C	17	Infantry,	Nov. 13,	1863	"
3127	Strout, Elias	"	C	17	"	July 19,	1863	"
3160	Trowbridge, John	"	B	10	"	Sept. 17,	1862	Removed from Antietam battlefield.
3176	Towle, Ezra	"	G	10	"	Sept. 17,	1862	"
3208	Townsend, Thomas	"	I	20	"	July 12,	1863	Removed from Funkstown.
3143	Turney, Enoch B.	"		7	"	Oct. 24,	1862	Removed from Frederick.
3130	Thompson, Asa L.	"		4	"	Dec. 27,	1862	"
3152	Unknown—Maine			20				Removed from Antietam battlefield.
3153	"			10				"
3175	"			10				"
3202	"			10		Sept. 18,	1862	"
3203	"			10				"
3204	"			10				"
3295	"			7				"
3129	Witham, James A.	Private,	A	16	"	July 20,	1863	Removed from Frederick.
3157	Wentworth, Charles H.	"	H	10	"	Sept. 30,	1862	Removed from Antietam battlefield.
3163	Washburn, Martin B.	"	C	20	"	Sept. 17,	1862	"
3178	Washburn, Daniel M.	"	A	19	"	Oct. 27,	1862	"
3209	Webb, Charles W.	"	C	5	"	Oct. 17,	1862	Removed from Frederick.
3144	White, Henry	"	G	1 Cavalry.		Oct. 30,	1862	"
3142	Young, Nelson	"		2 Battery,		Oct. 21,	1862	"
3145	York, William H.	"	B	7 Infantry,		Nov. 1,	1862	"
3135						Nov. 15,	1862	"

ANTIETAM NATIONAL CEMETERY.

MARYLAND.

Headst'e No.	NAME	Rank	Company	Regime't	Arm of Service	Date of Death			REMARKS
2572	Barr, Robert	Corporal,	F	1	P. H. B. Inf'y,	Aug.	28,	1864	Removed from Weverton.
2575	Barnes, David	Private,	K	1	Cavalry,	Aug.	5,	1864	"
2588	Brogunier, David	"		1	P. H. Brigade				Removed from Point of Rocks.
2469	Bunce, J. H.	"	H	2	"	June	13,	1864	Removed from Frederick, residence E. Shore.
2455	Brown, George	Corporal,	L	1	"	Aug.	4,	1864	Removed from Frederick.
2450	Bufler, Edward W.	Private,	B	1	Artillery,				Removed from Williamsport.
2416	Barker, John D.	Corporal,	E	3	P. H. B. Inf y,	July	9,	1864	Removed from Frederick.
2441	Bryne, James O.	"	K	1	Infantry.	Feb.	20,	1862	"
2432	Boyd, James	"	H	1	P. H. B. Inf y,				"
4227	Benner, Daniel	"	A	1	"	April	24,	1882	Rem'd from Lutheran graveyard, Sharpsburg.
2584	Caldwell, W. P.	"	A	1	"				Removed from Point of Rocks.
2597	Clazey, W.	Private,	F	1	"	April	2,	1854	Age 32.—Removed from Frederick.
2440	Clark, Enoch	Corporal,	A	4	"	Feb.	17,	1852	Removed from Frederick.
2563	Deshields, William	Private,	K	1	Cav	Aug.	5,	1864	Killed in action at Keedysville.
2578	Dorsey, David	"	K	1	Inf y.	Mar.	8,	1864	Removed from Weverton.
2451	Dove, Henry	"	B	7	Infantry,	Jan.	23,	1863	Age 24.—Removed from Hagerstown.
2438	Deincher, David H.	"	A	2	P. H. B.	Sept.	30,	1854	Died at Clarysville of wounds received from
2437	Delaney, Daniel	"	B	1	P. H. B. Cav.	Jan.	5,	1865	[his own gun. Removed from Clarysville.
2591	Flintham, George L.	Sergeant,	D	5		Oct.	24,	1862	Removed from Frederick.
2592	Friend, F. A.	Private,	K	3	P. H. B. Inf'y,	Dec.	23,	1862	"
2594	Fessmeyer, Joseph	"	A	6		July	8,	1863	Age 40.—Removed from Frederick.
2436	Friend, Elijah	"	"			Aug.	24,	1864	Removed from Clarysville.
2427	Frazee, Jonathan	"	_	2					Removed from Cumberland.
2429	Facenbaker, William	"	G	2					"
2468	Gosnell, Moses A.	"	C	1		June	24,	1864	Removed from Frederick.
2459	Gift, Martin Van Buren	"	A	1					Removed from Antietam.
2443	Gant, John F.	"	F	1					Removed from Frederick.
2442	Glass, William H.	"	K	1		Jan.	21,	1862	"
2562	Hipper, John			1					Removed from Antietam.
2569	Huggins, J. E.			3	"				Removed from Boonesboro'.
2573	Hanson, Edward	Sergeant,	K	2	Eastern Shore				Removed from Weverton.

DESCRIPTIVE LIST.   49

No.	Name	Rank	Co.	Regiment	Date	Year	Remarks
2580	Hayne, Mathews	Private,	E	2 Infantry,	Dec. 28,		Removed from Weverton.
2595	Harderson, George	"	G	3 P. H. B. Inf'y,	Sept. 6,	1863	Age 32—Removed from Frederick.
2465	Harmison, J. F.	"	E	1 "	Sept. 11,	1864	Removed from Frederick.
2464	Heavener, Robert	"	L	3 "		1864	"
2447	Horner, John	"	F		April 29,	1861	"
2445	Hardy, Abraham	"	H	1		1864	
2430	Hitchings, Charles	"	C	2	Mar. 18,	1863	Removed from Cumberland.
2448	Jenkins, David	"		3 Cole's Cavalry			Removed from Frederick.
2586	Keefe, Michael					1862	Removed from Point of Rocks.
2579	Keibler, Henry	Sergeant,	E	2 Cole's battal.	June 10,	1866	Removed from Weverton.
2590	Kerns, John J.	Private,	B	3 P. H. B. Inf'y.	Dec. 31,	1862	Age 32—Removed from Clearspring.
2593	Krobb, John	"	C	2		1862	Removed from Frederick.
2458	Kelly, William						Removed from Antietam.
2424	Kennedy, James	Corporal,	H	5 Infantry,	Oct. 1,	1862	Removed from Cumberland.
2461	Kohlman, Charles	Private,	E	19 "			Removed from Fred-rick.
2568	Love, James	"	A	9 "	May 3,	1864	Removed from Boonesboro'.
2472	Luders, Ludwig	"	K		June 22,	1864	Removed from Frederick.
2467	Lutz, Frederick	"		2 "			
2456	Lucart, Christian	"	D	2 "			Removed from Antietam.
2431	Laquie, Abraham	"		1 P. H. B. Cav.	July 5,	1864	Removed from Bloomington.
2471	Mentzer, F.	"		2 "			Removed from Frederick.
2561	Means, John	"		3 P. H. B. Inf'y,			Removed from Antietam.
2581	Maloney, Joseph	"	K	1 "			"
2553	McGuoy, ___						Removed from Berlin.
2596	Murray, Otto C.	"	H	1 Infantry,	May 29,	1864	Age 19—Removed from Frederick.
2473	Manley, M.	"	K	1 P. H. B. Cav.	May 12,	1864	Removed from Frederick.
2470	McAllister, Daniel	"	G	3 Infantry,	July 20,	1864	"
2462	Merling, George	"	G	9 "	Sept.	1852	
2439	McKeldin, Edward	"	A	2 "			
2425	Murphy, Patrick	"	F	7 "	Oct. 18,	1864	Removed from Clarysville.
4229	Miller, Levi	"	E				Removed from Frederick, Md., Dec. 10, '88.
2577	Noble, Gary L.	"	K	8 P. H. B.	Jan. 9,	1865	Age 25 years—Removed from Weverton.
2444	Neibergal, Lewis W.	"	K	1 P. H. B. Cav.	Mar. 25,	1854	Removed from Frederick.
2599	Pollman, William	"	H		June 26,	1862	"
2466	Powell, Abraham	"	B	3	Sept.	1864	
2567	Rooney, Michael	"	F				Removed from Smoketown.
2428	Rose, William M.	"	E	2 P. H. B.		1862	Removed from Cumberland.
4231	Reed, Francis C.	"	G	7 Infantry,			Removed from Hagerstown, Md. Dec. 17, '89.

ANTIETAM NATIONAL CEMETERY.

MARYLAND—CONTINUED.

Headst'e No.	NAME.	Rank.	Company	Regiment	Arm of Service.	Date of Death.	REMARKS.
2566	Schwartz, Frederick	Private,	A	6	Infantry,	Feb. 28, 1863	Removed from Smoketown.
2589	Shepard, John	"	G	7	"	Mar. 26, 1862	Removed from Clearspring.
2598	Simons, John A.	Sergeant,	F	3	"	Aug. 16, 1864	Removed from Frederick.
2460	Sullivan, John	Private,	A	1	P. H. B. Inf'y,		Removed from Antietam.
2457	Stewart, H. H.	Sergeant,	B	2	"		"
2571	Turner, Alexander	Private,	A	8	"		Removed from Boonesboro'.
2576	Tucker, Samuel	"	E	2	"	Oct. 31, 1863	Rem'd from Weverton. From Eastern Shore.
2463	Turner, R. H.	"	K	1	"	Sept. 3, 1862	Removed from Frederick.
2454	Thomas, John	"	C	6	Drummer,	Aug. 5, 1864	Killed in action at Keedysville.
2433	Trott, Geo.	"		1	P. H. B. Inf'y,	June 30, 1864	Killed at Maryland Heights. From Balto.
2564	Ulrick, W. F.	"		1	"		Removed from Antietam.
2570	Unknown,			1	"		
2582	"			1	"		
2587	"			1	"		
2588	"			1	"		
2449	"			1	"		
2452	"			1	Cole's Cavalry	Aug. 5, 1864	Killed in action at Keedysville.
2560	Watson, James	Sergeant,	K	1	"	July 26, 1864	Killed in action at Falling Waters.
2565	Wengert, Frederick	Private,	E		P. H. B. Inf'y,		Removed from Weverton.
2574	Wiles, Jacob F.	"	A	1	"		Removed from Antietam.
2453	Watson, Robert	"	B	1	Artillery,	Mar. 6, 1865	Removed from Clarysville.
2135	William, E. Van	"	B	2	"		Removed from Cumberland.
2434	Whitacker, John N.	"		3	P. H. B.		"
2426	Warnich, Andrew L.						

MASSACHUSETTS.

889	Adams, ——	Private,	F	21	Infantry,	Sept. 24,	1862	Removed from Antietam battlefield.
894	Austin, C. H.	"	F	18	"	Oct. 10,	1862	Age 26 years—Died of disease.
980	Adams, William F.	Corporal,	E	15	"	Aug. 17,	1864	Removed from Smoketown.
956	Arnold, Amassa	Private,	C	3	Cavalry,	Nov. 20,	1862	Removed from Weverton.
1028	Annis, Stelman S.	"	B	2	Infantry,	Oct. 7,	1862	Removed from Frederick.
1056	Adams, George	"	E	15	"	Sept. 20,	1862	" [moved from Antietam.
888	Brandage, Levi A.	"	F	35	"	Oct. 15,	1862	Died of wounds received at Antietam. Re-
986	Brown, S. H.	"	L	15	"	Nov. 17,	1863	Age 19—Died of disease.
981	Butler, Henry	"	C	19	"	Oct. 5,	1862	Removed from Smoketown.
977	Bryant, Daniel W.	"	D	34	"	July 30,	1852	Removed from Weverton.
966	Barry, Patrick	"	H	2	"	Aug. 14,	1864	Died of wounds, at Weverton.
1046	Butler, A. H.	"	F	34	"	Dec. 28,	1864	Removed from Frederick.
1047	Bowers, W. J.	"	I	2	Cavalry,	June 3,	1864	Died of Disease at Frederick.
1076	Bent, Henry	"		32	Infantry		1864	Age 19—Removed from Clarysville.
892	Carey, James	"	G	1	Battery,	Sept. 17,	1862	Removed from Antietam battlefield,
901	Cassidy, Francis	"		19	"			" "
1000	Clark, John W.	"	E	35	Infantry,	Oct. 4,	1862	Age 42—Rem'd from Antietam battlefield.
987	Cox, Richard H.	"	D	17	"	Sept. 22,	1862	Age 30—Died of wounds.
1015	Craig, Wm. H.	"	D	37	"			Removed from Hagerstown.
1016	Collier, Darius	"	D	2	"	Oct. 21,	1862	Died of disease at Hagerstown.
1021	Calvin, Frederick	"	D	19	"	May 26,	1862	Age 19—Removed from Frederick.
1032	Chandler, Adoniram	"	L	20	"	Jan. 3,	1864	Died of disease at Frederick.
1033	Chadwick, G. W.	"	C	2	Cavalry,	Jan. 16,	1864	Removed from Frederick.
1050	Coligan, W.	"	B	2	Infantry,	Sept. 28,	1864	" "
1060	Cady, J. D.	"	C	2	"	Sept. 25,	1862	" "
1067	Carey, James	"		34	"	Feb. 14,	1862	Removed from Cumberland.
1072	Crouch, Edwin L.	"	L	32	"	May 21,	1864	Died of wounds.
1079	Copp, A. J.	"	C	35	"	Unknown		Removed from Lutheran Graveyard.
893	Clay, Thomas	Sergeant,	K	21	"			Removed from Antietam battlefield.
990	Davis, George W.	Private,	E	15	"	Sept. 22,	1862	Clappsville, Mass., rem'd from Hagerstown.
954	Davis, Alfred W.	Corporal,	B	22	"	Oct. 4,	1862	Age 41—Died of wounds. Rem'd from Fred'k.
1058	Davis, George	"	G	24	"	June 15,	1864	Removed from Clarysville.
1077	Dickson, John E.	Private,	I	2	"	Feb. 22,	1862	Removed from Frederick, Md.
1063	Eastman, Dunbar	Corporal,	G	2	"	July 20,	1862	" "
1073	Estes, Samuel S.	Private,	M	2	Cavalry,	June 15,	1865	Removed from Clarysville.

52 ANTIETAM NATIONAL CEMETERY.

MASSACHUSETTS—Continued.

Headst'e No.	NAME.	Rank.	Company	Regiment	Arm of Service.	Date of Death.		REMARKS.
976	Fitz, James	Private,	G	12	Infantry,	Nov. 6,	1862	Removed from Smoketown.
951	Fleming, Thomas	"	L	28	"	Sept. 17,	1862	Removed from Hagerstown.
900	Grant, Alex.	"		19	"			Removed from Antietam battlefield.
936	Gutemuth, Frederick	"	B	20	"	Sept. 17,	1862	" "
982	Getchell, H. D.	"	C	15	"	Oct. 14,	1862	Removed from Smoketown.
965	Gaylord, Albert H.	"	D	34	"	July 30,	1864	Died of disease. Removed from Weverton.
961	Greenlaw, T. M.	"	F	26	"			Removed from Weverton.
960	Griffith, Henry P.	"	A	35	"	Nov. 13,	1863	Age 28, died of disease. Rem'd f'm Weverton.
904	Harwood, E. O.	"	E	20	"	Sept. 17,	1862	Removed from Antietam battlefield.
938	Hurd, Hiram A.	"	F	12	"	Sept. 17,	1862	Killed in action. Removed from Antietam.
1007	Holden, Hollis	"	K	13	"	Sept. 17,	1862	Age 44—Removed from Antietam.
1001	Hall, A. P.	"	H	13	"	Sept. 17,	1862	Age 25—Removed from Antietam.
984	Hewins, Henry	"	D	2	"	Nov. 29,	1862	Removed from Smoketown.
967	Hodde, John H.	"	E	28	"			Removed from Middletown.
959	Hogg, John	"		2	"	Mar. 13,	1864	Age 24—Removed from Weverton.
957	Hay, Henry C.	"		1	"			Removed from Weverton.
983	Hazen, Jacob F.	"	C	19	"	Sept. 17,	1862	Removed from Smoketown.
1017	Hill, John O.	"			"			Removed from Hagerstown.
1022	Hazeltine, Moses	"	C	12	"	Oct. 16,	1862	Removed from Frederick.
1035	Hennessy, Jere.	"	H	2	"	Mar. 11,	1863	"
1041	Hitchcock, Alfred	"	D	37	"	Aug. 7,	1864	Died of wounds. Removed from Frederick.
1042	Hurley, Luke	"	G	30	"	Aug. 30,	1864	Removed from Frederick.
1043	Harvey, James	"	K	26	"	Sept. 16,	1864	"
1055	Hayden, Frank L.	"	H	15	"	Sept. 27,	1862	"
891	Ingalls, M. M.	"	H	22	"	Oct. 24,	1862	Age 20—Removed from Frederick.
972	Jones, Edward	"	G	2	"	Nov. 17,	1862	Age 34—Removed from Antietam battlefield.
1054	Jones, William M.	"	D	13	"	Aug. 26,	1862	Died of disease.
955	Kelsey, C. J.	"	B	37	"	Aug. 17,	1864	Removed from Weverton.
890	Knowlton, C. C.	"	P	22	"	Oct. 13,	1862	Age 21, died of wounds. Rem'd f'm Antietam.
903	Kehr, George W.	"	K	20	"	Sept. 17,	1862	Removed from Antietam.
934	Keith, F. H.	Sergeant,		20	"			"

DESCRIPTIVE LIST.

No.	Name	Rank	Co.	Age	Regiment	Date	Year	Remarks
1068	King, Warren H.	Private,	G	2	2 Infantry,	May 29,	1852	Removed from Frederick.
895	Lewis, James	"		20	"	Oct. 18,	1862	Removed from Antietam battlefield.
899	Leach, Edward	Sergeant,		19	"	April 19,	1865	Removed from Hagerstown.
958	——, L——	"		2	"	April 27,	1865	"
1020	Lynch, J. R.	"	G	2	"	Sept. 17,	1862	Removed from Frederick.
1023	Leonard, Charles	Private,	L	21	"	Sept. 17,	1862	Removed from Frederick.
1075	Legrass, Theophilus	"	E	30	"	Sept. 24,	1862	Removed from Clarysville.
1078	Loud, Benjamin	"	E	2	Cavalry,	Oct. 5,	1852	Age 18—Removed from Clarysville.
898	McQuestion, Clinton	"	D	20	"	July 30,	1862	Removed from Antietam battlefield.
905	McDonough, John	"	F	20	"		1864	"
988	McNally, R.	"	E	28	"			"
973	Mores, Robert R.	"	C	15	"	Oct. 25,	1862	Removed from Smoketown.
971	Moran, George	"	L	34	"	Dec. 28,	1852	Died of sunstroke. Rem'd f'm Antietam field.
969	Mellen, Sidney	"				Nov. 12,		Removed from Middletown.
964	Murray, William F.	"	K	32	Infantry,	Oct. 5,	1863	Removed from Weverton.
1025	Murphy, James B.	"	E	12	"	Feb. 19,	1862	Removed from Frederick.
1031	McCarthy, John	"	K	2	"	Aug. 24,	1862	Age 22—Died of wounds. Rem'd from Fred'k.
1040	McLaughlin, James	"	C	9	"	Sept. 17,	1864	Removed from Frederick.
1061	McLay, James	"		2	"	Dec. 15,	1862	Removed from Clarysville.
1069	Means, James H.	"	D	12	"	Jan. 20,	1862	Removed from Hagerstown.
1070	Mahan, Walter	"	E	34	"	Sept. 17,	1853	Age 38—Died of disease. Rem'd f'm Fred'k.
953	Nicholson, Francis N.	"	G	28	"	Sept. 17,	1852	Wounded Sept. 17, 1862.
1030	Nash, Francis J.	"	B	35	"	Oct. 14,	1862	Removed from Antietam battlefield.
1034	Nulty, John	"	C	28	"	Nov. 19,	1862	Removed from Smoketown.
896	Perry, Charles	"	F	15	"	Mar. 20,	1863	Removed from Frederick.
975	Pool, E. G.	"	G	12	"	Aug. 14,	1864	"
1029	Pike, George H.	"	J	37	"	Mar. 6,	1865	"
1037	Pickett, Thomas	"	I	29	"	Mar. 25,	1865	"
1045	Partenhimer, William	"	H	34	"	Dec. 26,	1861	"
1052	Pazant, Lewis	"	C	2	"			
1053	Palmer, Thomas	Corporal,	B	2	"			
1062	Pierce, James	Private,	H	2	"			Removed from Clarysville.
1071	Paltong, John	"	D	3	Cavalry,	Sept. 17,	1862	Removed from Hagerstown.
952	Quinn, Michael	"	K	28	Infantry,	S'pt. 17,	1862	Removed from Antietam battlefield.
902	Riley, John	"	H	20	"	Sept. 17,	1862	Age 23, died of wounds. Rem'd f'm Antietam.
989	Robbins, C. H.	"	H	35	"	Oct. 12,	1862	Age 25—Removed from Antietam.
985	Reed, Silas L.	"	D	35	"	Oct. 27,	1862	Removed from Antietam.
978	Renich, Prescott	"	G	2	"			Removed from Smoketown.

MASSACHUSETTS—CONTINUED.

Head'e No.	NAME.	Rank.	Company	Reg'm't	Arm of Service.	Date of Death.	REMARKS.
1038	Reed, Israel S.	Private,	I	2	Infantry,	Mar. 16, 1863	Removed from Frederick.
935	Ross, J. C.	"	L	19	"		Removed from Antietam battlefield.
1048	Riley, T. O.	Corporal,	C	3	Cavalry,	Oct. 11, 1864	Removed from Frederick.
1049	Rhodes, Charles	Private,	?	?	"	Oct. 29, 1864	"
897	Schneider, Jacob	"	B	20	Infantry,		Removed from Antietam battlefield,
979	Shilling, John	"	B	20	"	Sept. 20, 1862	Removed from Smoketown.
974	Smith, Granville H.	Corporal,	B	12	"	Oct. 20, 1862	"
970	Shiran, George S.	Private,	E	36	"		Removed from Middletown.
968	Sloan, J. V.	"	E	35	"		"
962	Shook, George L.	Corporal,	C	37	"	Oct. 18, 1864	Removed from Weverton. Died of wounds.
1018	Sears, Urbane	Private,	H	37	"	Nov. 12, 1862	Removed from Hagerstown. Died of disease.
1024	Snow, Alfred J.	"	G	13	"	Oct. 19, 1862	Removed from Frederick.
1026	Sullivan, Simon	"	H	15	"	Oct. 21, 1862	"
1044	Shiffer, John F.	Corporal,	F	2	Cavalry,	Sept. 18, 1864	"
1064	Stevens, Alfred	Private,	G	2	Infantry,	Mar. 30, 1862	"
1074	Stropper, Sebastian	"	M	30	"	Dec. 4, 1864	Removed from Clarysville.
1036	Schwarneeberger, John	"	K	20	"	Mar. 6, 1863	Removed from Frederick. [disease.
1027	Treadwell, Nathaniel C.	"	L	35	"	Oct. 25, 1862	Removed from Frederick. Age 19—Died of
937	Treen, J. S.	"	E	2	"	Sept. 17, 1862	Removed from Antietam battlefield.
1059	Westgate, Joseph	"	F	29	"	Unknown	"
963	Wilber, Winfield S.	"	E	2	Cavalry,	Sept. 18, 1864	Removed from Weverton,
1051	Walther, Jacob	"	E	2	"	Oct. 17, 1864	Removed from Frederick.
1065	Wallace, J. A.	"	B	2	Infantry,	April 9, 1862	"
1057	Wintzer, Armond	"	L	42	"	Oct. 14, 1862	"
1039	Young, William	"	D	19	"	July 6, 1863	"
28	Unknown—Massachusetts.			15		Sept. 17, 1862	Removed from Antietam battlefield.
34	Unknown—Massachusetts.						"

MICHIGAN.

No.	Name	Rank	Co.	Regt.	Arm	Date	Year	Remarks
2375	Arge, James	Corporal,	E,	1	Cavalry,	Sept. 18,	1864	Removed from Weverton, Md. [at Fred'k.
2400	Ackerly, Cussander	Private,	G,	8	Infantry,	Dec. 3,	1862	Removed from Fred'k. Died of wounds rec'd
2523	Buck, Luman	"	F,	4	"	Sept. 17,	1862	Killed in battle. From Lawrence County.
2546	Blanchard, Simon F.	"	D,	17	"	Nov. 1,	1862	Died of wounds. From Kalamazoo.
2556	Bennett, Benjamin	"	I,	7	"	Aug. 9,	1863	Removed from Frederick—Age 17.
2557	Bennett, George A.	"	H,	3	"	Aug. 10,	1863	Died of disease at Frederick—Age 24. Sandy Hook.
2389	Baker, ———	"						
2406	Bragg, George E.	"	C,	7	"	Oct. 2,	1862	Frederick.
2521	Clyce, Jacob	"	C,	8	"	Sept. 19,	1862	Died of wounds at Antietam. From Cos.
2522	Catlin, George W.	"	L,	16	"	Oct. 26,	1862	Died of typhoid fever, near Sharpsburg.
2510	Carney, Mason	"		17	"	Sept. 14,	1862	Killed at South Mountain. From Dundee.
2486	Clements, ———	"			"		1862	Removed from Middletown.
2483	Curtis, Richard	"	E,	20	"	Nov. 8,	1862	Died of disease at Weverton.
2379	C———, Peter M.	"		17	"		"	"
2382	Collins, Samuel	"	A,	7	"	Sept. 24,	1862	Died of disease at Antietam. From Salivac.
2393	Crane, Newman	"	H,	17	"	Oct. 14,	1862	Died of wounds at South Mountain. Fayette.
2398	Chaffer, Wilbur E.	"	L,	17	"	Oct. 31,	1862	Died of wounds at Antietam. Kalamazoo.
2415	Clark, George	"	G,	6	Cavalry,			Killed accidentally at Boonsboro. Lansing.
2516	Deshliter, Basil L.	"	D,	7	Infantry,	Oct. 9,	1862	Died of wounds at Antietam. From Monroe.
2484	Dennis, Richard	"	D,	17	"	Oct. 2,	1862	Died of disease at Weverton.
2384	Darling, Ansel J.	"	G,	17	"	Sept. 17,	1862	Killed at Antietam. From Backner.
2402	Dickinson, Thomas	Sergeant,	E,	6	Cavalry,	Mar. 8,	1865	Died of disease at Frederick. From Bashnell.
2409	Dodds, William	Private,	F,	1	"	Feb. 7,	1862	Died of disease at Frederick. From Adrian.
2401	Ebert, John	"	A,	4	Infantry	Nov. 30,	1862	Died of disease at Frederick. From Lapeer.
2481	Fisher, Albert H.	"	H,	7	Cavalry,	Aug. 21,	1864	Died of disease at Frederick. From Barry.
2394	Fliece, Henry	"	F,	7	Infantry,	Oct. 19,	1862	Died of wounds at Antietam. From Haughton.
2412	Finch, Richard G.	Sergeant,	D,	7	Cavalry,	April 13,	1862	Died of typhoid fever at Frederick. Duplain.
2573	Grimes, Micah M.	"	M,	1	"	Sept. 3,	1864	Died of wounds. From Niles.
2396	Gates, Lawrence	Private,	K,	7	"	Oct. 20,	1862	Removed from Frederick.
2482	Gilbert, E. J.	"						
2392	Gillett, George M.	"	B,	1	Infantry,	July 31,	1863	Died of wounds at Hagerstown. Margette.
2550	Hill, Charles L.	"	K,	7	"	Oct. 17,	1862	Died of wounds at Antietam. From Burr Oak.
2554	Hawkins, J. W.	"	D,	7	"	July 20,	186?	Removed from Frederick—Age 22
2513	Hovey, Spencer H.	"	D,	17	"	Sept. 14,	186?	Killed at South Mountain. From Augusta.
2374	H———, Peter	"	A,	1	Cavalry,	Aug. 2,	1864	Removed from Weverton.
2395	Higgins, Henry	"	G,	8	Infantry,	Oct. 11,	1862	Died of wounds rec'd at Fred'k. Lenawee.

ANTIETAM NATIONAL CEMETERY.

MICHIGAN—Continued.

Hendst's No.	NAME.	Rank.	Company	Reg'ment	Arm of Service.	Date of Death.		REMARKS.
2419	Henderson, Lyman M.	Private,	B	1	Engineers,	Apr. 4,	1865	Removed from Frederick.
2420	Harrold, John L.	"	G	2	Cavalry,	Mar. 9,	1865	"
2476	Harrington, Morey	"	B	1	"	Jan. 12,	1865	Died at Frederick. From Dexter.
2501	Irwin, Robert C.	"	E	17	Infantry,	Sept. 17,	1862	Killed at Antietam. From Brooklyn.
2377	Jott, Harrison	"	I	1	Cavalry,	Aug. 31,	1864	Died of wounds, at Weverton. From Aurelius.
2551	Kuhnel, George	"	F	1	Infantry,	Oct. 10,	1862	Died of wounds at Antietam. F'm Haughton.
2405	Kirk, George M.	"	B	"	"	Sept. 14,	1862	Killed at South Mountain. From Pipestone.
2422	Keis, John	"	E		Cavalry,	May 12,	1862	Removed from Clarysville.
2399	Lauclause, Gustavus	"	D	7		Oct. 30,	1862	Removed from Frederick.
2555	Lee, Bristol A.	"	C	24	Infantry,	Aug. 2,	1862	Died of Disease at Frederick. F'm Plymouth.
2509	Lilly, David V.	"	I	17	"	Sept. 14,	1862	Killed at South Mountain. From Leighton.
2407	Lewis, Daniel S.	"	L	7	"	Dec. 2,	1862	Died of disease at Frederick. F'm Kalamazoo.
2408	Lowe, Isaac N.	"	M	1	Cavalry,	Jan. 5,	1862	" " Waterszeit.
2404	Lampson, V. R.	"	E	7	Infantry,	Sept. 20,	1862	Removed from Frederick.
2552	Manning, Albert	"	F	7	"	Nov. 10,	1862	Died of wounds at Antietam. F'm Haughton.
2518	McCullen, Charles H.	"	G	7	"	Oct. 10,	1862	" " Lapeer.
2507	McMartin, Daniel E.	"	D	17	"	Dec. 14,	1862	Killed at South Mountain. From Kalamazoo.
2502	McKinster, Alexander	"	E	17	"	Sept. 14,	1862	" " Sheboygan.
2381	Mundle, John	"	B	8	"	Nov. 21,	1862	Removed from Sandy Hook. From Dallas.
2410	Morgan, Dorr	"	B	1	Cavalry,	April 7,	1862	Died at Frederick. From Dexter.
2421	McPherson, Finley	"	F	6	"	May 5,	1865	Died of disease at Clarysville. From Lapeer.
2517	O'Niel, John	"	G	7	Infantry,	Oct. 7,	1862	Died of wounds at Antietam. From Lapeer.
2511	O'Neal, Samuel	"	D	17	"			Removed from South Mountain.
2485	Ordinary, Elijah	"	A	17	"	Nov. 12,	1863	Died of typhoid fever Weverton. F'm Adman.
2414	Orcutt, George	"	F	1	Cavalry,	Jan. 30,	1862	Died at Frederick. From Lapeer.
2524	Palmer, George	"	B	7	Infantry,	Sept. 25,	1862	Died of wounds Antietam. F'm Ingham Co.
2547	Powers, Nathan S.	"	D	17	"	Oct. 24,	1862	Died at Big Spring Hosp. From Johnstown.
2553	Piper, Frederick	"	F	7	"	Jan. 28,	1863	Died of disease at Frederick. F'm Houghton.
2512	Palmetier, Almeron	"	D	17	"	Sept. 14,	1862	Killed at South Mountain. From Johnstown.
2376	Pratt, David S.	"	C	17	"	Dec. 12,	1862	Died of disease at Weverton. From Ovid.
2403	Patterson, Andrew	"	I	1209	Engineers,	June 11,	1865	Removed from Frederick.

DESCRIPTIVE LIST.

No.	Name	Rank	Co.	Reg.	Branch	Date	Year	Remarks
2416	Pierson, Henry	Private,	D	5	Cavalry,	Feb.	1864	Died of disease at Clarysville. F'm Wayne Co.
2423	Palmer, John L.	"	"	7	"	June 5,	1865	Removed from Clarysville.
2179	Reynolds, Hugh H.	"	F	1	"	Oct. 1,	1861	Died at Frederick. From Detroit.
2474	Robinson, James	"	M	7	"	Mar. 4,	1865	Removed from Clarysville.
2391	Rogers, Remis	"	P	6	"			Removed from Hagerstown.
2548	Scully, Thomas	"	G	17	Infantry,	Dec. 17,	1862	Died of wounds at Antietam. From Jackson.
2558	Soule, John W.	Corporal,	D	6	Cavalry,	Sept. 8,	1863	Killed in action at Boonsboro'. F'm Cohoctah.
2519	Spoth, Andrew	Private,	F	7	Infantry,	Feb. 10,	1863	Died of wounds at Antietam. F'm Haughton.
2515	Smith, Wilbur F.	"	D	17	"	Sept. 14,	1862	Killed at South Mountain. From Cooper.
2175	Stant, James B.	"	I	6	Cavalry,	Feb. 23,	1865	Died at Frederick.
2380	Smith, John W.	"	K	20	Infantry,	Nov. 19,	1862	Died of disease at Weverton. From Sylvan.
2390	Sears, James	"	M	6	Cavalry,	April 19,	1865	Died at Boonsboro'.
2397	Smith, Charles R.	"	G	19	Infantry	Oct. 15,	1862	Removed from Frederick.
2525	Seely, T. B.	"	B	7	"	Sept. 17,	1862	Removed from Antietam battlefield. From Olive.
2413	Seeley, W. S.	"	F	1	Cavalry.	Feb. 13,	1862	Removed from Frederick. [Jackson, Mich.
2492	Sears, Eli	"	K	17	"	Sept. 4,	1862	Killed at South Mountain. F'm Jackson, Mich.
2411	Smith, William M.	"	G	7	"	Jan. 25,	1862	Died at Frederick.
2418	Stanton, Chancy W.	"	C	8	Infantry,	June 6,	1865	Removed from Clarysville.
2520	Tallman, Henry S.	"	L	7	Cavalry,	Sept. 17,	1862	Died of wounds at Antietam. F'm Aliedon.
2477	Turner, D.	"				Dec. 22,	1864	Removed from Frederick.
2388	Taylor,	"						Removed from Sandy Hook.
2526	Temison, James	"						Removed from Antietam battlefield.
2500	Vanderburg, Delas W.	"	H	7	Infantry,	Sept. 14,	1862	Killed at South Mountain. From Olive.
2543	Wray, Orrin	"	B	17	Cavalry,	Sept. 2,	1864	Died of wounds. From Niles.
2549	Watson, Colbert R.	"		17	"			Removed from Antietam battlefield.
2559	Windsor, William W.	"	F	3	"			Removed from Clarysville.
2514	Ward, Benjamin	"	D	17	Infantry,	Sept. 14,	1862	Killed at South Mountain. From Pipestone.
2417	Wolf, Solomon	"	L	1	Cavalry,			Removed from Cumberland.
2480	Watkins, Richard	"	M	5	"	Sept. 8,	1864	Died of disease at Frederick. From Leonulas.
2478	Wheeler, Alonzo	"	G	1	"	Oct. 17,	1864	Died at Frederick.
2488	Walker, Stephen B.	"	D	8	Infantry,	Nov. 2,	1862	Died at Middletown. From Holland.
2487	Weeks, Charles L.	"	I	17	"	Sept. 28,	1862	Died of wounds at South Mountain.
2378	Yocum, Malon	"		17	"			Removed from Antietam battlefield.
	27 Unknown—Michigan.			20	"			Removed from Weverton
	10 Unknown—Michigan.			17	"			Removed from South Mountain battlefield.

ANTIETAM NATIONAL CEMETERY.

MINNESOTA.

Hendsr'e No.	NAME.	Rank.	Company	Regiment	Arm of Service.	Date of Death.	REMARKS.
3025	Abbott, David P.	Private,	F	1	Infantry,	Sept. 17, 1862	Killed in action. Removed from Antietam.
3021	Bowman, John W.	"	C	1	Battery,	June 26, 1865	Removed from Frederick.
3020	Brown, Joseph T.	"	E	1	Infantry,	Sept. 30, 1862	" "
3026	Boyce, George E.	"	—	—	"	—	Removed from Antietam.
3028	Cornman, Oscar L.	Corporal,	B	1	"	Sept. 17, 1852	Killed in action. Removed from Antietam.
3023	Goundry, John E.	Private,	B	1	"	Sept. 17, 1862	" "
3019	Hancock, J. O.	"	A	9	"	—	Removed from Westernport.
3022	Laird, Samuel	Sergeant,	G	1	"	Aug. 22, 1862	Killed in action. Removed from Frederick.
3027	McEwen, John	"	A	1	"	Sept. 17, 1862	Killed Sept. 17, 1862. Removed f'm Antietam.
3024	Milliken, M. B.	Private,	F	1	"	Sept. 17, 1862	Removed from Antietam battlefield.

NEW HAMPSHIRE.

Hendsr'e No.	NAME.	Rank.	Company	Regiment	Arm of Service.	Date of Death.	REMARKS.
2820	Barrington, Henry	Private,	F	9	Infantry,	Oct. 12, 1862	Age 23—Removed from Antietam.
2800	Dearborn, Henry C.	"	L	12	"	Oct. 1, 1862	Died of disease. Removed from Antietam.
2818	Fullerton, James, Jr.	"	—	—	"	—	Removed from Antietam.
2811	Garland, John W.	"	H	9	"	Nov. 26, 1852	Died at Knoxville. Removed from Weverton.
2804	Howe, John	"	H	9	"	Oct. 10, 1862	Died Big S. Hospital. Rem'd from Antietam.
2809	Haselton, Enoch E.	Sergeant,	D	9	"	Oct. 17, 1862	Died of Wounds. Rem'd from Middletown.
2816	Holt, Abbott D.	Private,	G	9	"	Oct. 4, 1862	Died of disease S. Mt'n. Rem'd f'm Antiet'm.
2891	Hale, James P.	"	B	9	"	Oct. 1, 1863	Died at Frederick. Rem'd from Frederick.
2890	Hill, Elisha M.	"	—	5	"	Oct. 8, 1863	Removed from Frederick.
2810	Knights, W. S.	"	F	9	"	Nov. 30, 1862	Died at Frederick. Rem'd f'm Middletown.
2893	Kimball, William	"	K	12	"	Nov. 15, 1862	Died of disease. Removed from Frederick.
2801	Lovett, Oliver W.	"	A	6	"	Sept. 29, 1862	Died at Antietam. Removed from Antietam.
2812	Murphy, John	"	B	1	Cavalry,	Sept. 8, 1864	Died at S. Hook, Md. Rem'd f'm Weverton.
2819	Nichols, George F.	"	I	12	Infantry,	Oct. 21, 1862	Died at Knoxville, Md. Col. Marsh's reg't.*
2892	Page, Ira E.	"	A	12	"	July 3, 1863	Died at Frederick. Removed from Frederick.
2807	Quinn, Charles A.	"	F	5	"	Sept. 17, 1862	Died of wounds. Removed From Antietam.

*Removed from Antietam.

DESCRIPTIVE LIST.

No.	Name	Rank	Co.	Regt.	Date		Remarks
2805	Redington, J. P.	Private,	K	9 Infantry,	Oct. 20,	1862	Died of Disease. Removed from Antietam.
2808	Shaffer, Elie	"	G	2 Battery,	Dec. 3,	1862	Died at Smoketown. Rem'd f'm Smoketown.
2814	Trow, Josiah	"	G	6 Infantry,	Oct. 25,	1862	Died of disease. Removed from Smoketown.
2815	Trow, Charles P.	Corporal,	F	6 "	Nov. 19,	1862	Died of disease. Removed from Knoxville.
2817	Unknown—New Hampshire.	Private,			Nov. 9,	1862	Removed from Antietam.
2803	Winship, D. H.	"	F	12	Nov. 14,	1862	Died of wounds. Removed from Antietam.
2806	Waters, Sylvanus C.	"	F	9	Sept. 17,	1862	Killed at Antietam. Rem'd from Antietam.
2813	Woods, Alfred H.	"	B	9	Nov. 3,	1862	Died at Weverton. Removed from Weverton.
2802	Yates, William R.	"	B	5	Sept. 27,	1862	Died of wounds. Removed from Antietam.

NEW JERSEY.

No.	Name	Rank	Co.	Regt.	Date		Remarks
2779	Alpine, John	Private,	H	13 Infantry,	July 3,	1863	Removed from Antietam battle-field.
2920	Anderson, Henry A.	"	G	14 "	Dec. 30,	1862	Removed from Frederick.
2908	Arrants, William H.	"	D	14	July 6,	1863	Age 75—Removed from Frederick.
2926	Ackerson, John	"	I	15	Nov. 3,	1862	Removed from Frederick.
2905	Bates, Benjamin J.	Corporal,	I	14	Aug. 23,	1864	Died at Frederick. Rem'd f'm Frederick.
2993	Bates, Smith	Private,	E	14	April 12,	1863	Removed from Frederick—Age 23.
2924	Bayard, Cornelius	"	K	14	July 9,	1864	"
2927	Beany, John T.	"	A	14	July 23,	1864	"
2932	Blackwell, Benjamin D.	"	K	14	July 17,	1864	"
2928	Brown, William	"	E	2	Sept. 17,	1862	Killed in action. Removed from Antietam.
2781	Carroll, Samuel	"	K	10	Aug. 19,	1864	Removed from Weverton.
2797	Combs, Robert S.	"	K	14	Dec. 7,	1862	Removed from Frederick.
2999	Carver, Daniel	"	A	11	Dec. 29,	1862	Died at Frederick. Rem'd f'm Frederick.
2899	Conrow, Darling	"	F	13	Jan. 12,	1863	"
2896	Clayton, Isaac	Sergeant,	A	14	Jan. 5,	1863	"
2918	Coyle, James	Private,	I	14	July 23,	1864	"
2919	Cowell, John	"	L	10	Jan. 12,	1865	"
2931	Compton, John	"	K	13	Oct. 20,	1862	Age 21—Removed from Weverton.
2938	Crater, John	"		14	Nov. 16,	1862	Died at Frederick. Rem'd from Frederick.
2791	Demarest, Martin V. P.	"	C	14	July 9,	1864	"
2914	Dey, Austin A.	"	D	26	Nov. 6,	1862	Removed from Hagerstown.
2933	Darby, Greenleaf S.	"	G	14	Dec. 7,	1862	Died at Frederick. Removed f'm Frederick.
2798	Elwood, George	"	E	13	Dec. 1,	1862	Died at Sharpsburg, Md.
2911	Emily, Alonzo						
2778	Fitzgerald, John						

NEW JERSEY—Continued.

Headst'e No.	NAME.	Rank.	Company	Regiment	Arm of Service.	Date of Death.	REMARKS.
2910	Foley, M.	Private,	H	14	Infantry,	Nov. 28, 1862	Died at Frederick, Md.
2913	Grover, Samuel	"	F	14	"	Nov. 7, 1862	" " "
2900	Gammwell, Robert	"	K	13	"	Dec. 11, 1862	" " "
2934	Gibson, Isaac H.	"	A	14	"	July 19, 1864	" " "
2940	Heaton, Daniel	"	H	3	"		Removed from Cumberland.
2784	Hemberger, Andrew W.	"	K	2	"	Sept. 14, 1864	Killed in action at Burkettsville, Md.
2907	Hyers, Josiah	"	G	14	"	Dec. 11, 1864	Removed from Frederick.
2897	Havens, Edward	"	D	14	"	July 15, 1864	" " "
2925	Holloway, Samuel	"	G	14	"	Mar. 18, 1863	" " "
2930	Haveland, Charles H.	"	F	14	"	July 15, 1864	" " "
2788	Jansen, Herman	"	E	2	.	Oct. 1, 1862	
2922	Kelly, Patrick	"	H	14	"	April 13, 1863	Removed from Frederick.
2787	Lyudon, James P.	"	C	2	"	Sept. 14, 1862	Killed at Burkettsville, Md.
2912	Lesher, William	"	C	14	"	Nov. 18, 1862	Removed from Frederick.
2936	Lancaster, William R.	"	H	10	"	Sept. 15, 1864	" " "
2937	Looker, Thomas J.	Corporal,	C	14	"	Sept. 26, 1864	" " "
2780	McMonigle, John	Private,	C	2	"	Sept. 17, 1862	Killed in action at Antietam.
2785	Mullender, William	"	F	2	"		
2795	Miller, Carl	"	D	3	Cavalry,	Aug. 22, 1864	Removed from Sandy Hook, Md.
2796	McCully, Samuel	"	D	4	Infantry,	Nov. 9, 1864	Removed from Frederick.
2916	McDougall, John	"	H	11	"	Oct. 28, 1862	" " "
2904	Mclman, Charles	"	B	1	"	Oct. 31, 1862	" " "
2902	Montgomery, Benjamin F.	Corporal,	E	14	Musician,	Nov. 22, 1862	" " "
2929	Magee, J. V.	Private,	A	14	Infantry,	July 25, 1864	" " "
2793	Outwater, John W.	"	I	1	"	Sept. 16, 1862	Removed from Weverton.
2715	Parker, Charles	"	A	14	"	Nov. 8, 1862	Removed from Frederick.
2901	Patterson, Charles	"	K	14	"	Dec. 23, 1862	" " "
2895	Reynear, Theodore F.	"	F	14	Wagoner,	Dec. 28, 1862	" " "
2894	Rose, Samuel B.	"	F	14	Cavalry,	Feb. 8, 1863	" " "
2939	Reed, Jonathan	"	C	3	Infantry,		
2790	Smith, Merton L.	Sergeant,	F	13	"	Oct. 25, 1862	Removed from Weverton.

DESCRIPTIVE LIST.

2917	Schnell, Conrad	Sergeant,	H	1	Infantry,	Nov.	8,	1861	Removed from Hagerstown.
2921	Strout, Luke	"	K	14	"	Mar.	31,	1863	Removed from Frederick.
2935	Shores, William A. N.	"	D	14	"	"	"	1864	"
2941	Shuman, Emile	"	L	3	Cavalry,	July	9,	1865	Removed from Clarysville.
2923	Tice, Jonathan	"	F	14	Infantry,	April	21,	1863	Removed from Frederick.
2782	Unknown—New Jersey,	"		13	"				
2783	"	"		13	"				
2786	"	"							
2792	"	"							
2789	"	"	G	14	"	Dec.	5,	1862	"
2906	Van Brunt, Benjamin	"	E	14	"	Jan.	3,	1863	"
2898	Van Brunt, Jacob	"	K	15	"	Sept.	4,	1861	Removed from Weverton.
2794	Wilson, William	"	K	2	"	Nov.	16,	1862	Removed from Hagerstown.
2799	Williamson, Charles								

NEW YORK SECTION.

NEW YORK.

DESCRIPTIVE LIST.

Headst'e No.	NAME.	Rank.	Company	Regiment	Arm of Service.	Date of Death.	REMARKS.
71	Albriz, Fredoline	Private.	A	15	Cavalry,	July 10, 1854	Frederick, Md.
748	Adair, John B.	Corporal,	B	9	Infantry,	Unknown.	Removed from Antietam battlefield.
826	Adle, John H.	Private,	C	34	"	"	"
834	Allen, William	Sergeant,	G	42	"	"	"
540	Annis, Myron	Private,		1	N. Y. Battery,		
590	Adsit, James E.	"	F	97	Infantry,	Oct. 17, 1862	Removed from Smoketown.
616	Allen, George	"	D	105	"	Oct. 8, 1862	"
505	Avery, William	"	G	97	"	Oct. 25, 1862	"
285	Angus, Charles M.	"	A	5	Artillery	Aug. 16, 1864	Removed from Weverton.
303	Anthony, Lewis	"	H	165	Infantry,	Aug. 27, 1864	"
369	Austin, Jesse	"	D	122	"	Oct. 19, 1862	Removed from Hagerstown.
184	Applin, Uriah F.	"		151	"	July 9, 1863	Removed from Frederick.
63	Ackles, Franklin	"	A	9	Heavy Artil'y.	July 16, 1864	May be C. Acker.
137	Ames, Martin L.	"	H	6	Cavalry,	May 22, 1865	Removed from Frederick.
33	Averill, Franklin	Corporal,	E	21	"	Unknown,	Removed from Cumberland.
296	Algier, G. M.	Private,	F	43	Infantry,	Sept. 17, 1862	May be George M. Algier, Weverton.
766	Brown, Charles	"	B	103	"	"	Killed in action at Antietam.
790	Byrne, John	"	C	4	"	"	Removed from Antietam battlefield,
814	Bortle, Belden	"	L	108	"	"	"
817	Beckman, Franz	"	D	108	"	"	"
818	Brandt, Fred	"	B	7	"	"	May be Frank Brather.
819	Brayman, Samuel H.	"	F	61	"	"	Removed from Antietam battlefield.
833	Blabang, William	"	D	42	"	Sept. 17, 1862	"
845	Bailey, Henry	"	A	34	"	Unknown,	"
732	Beck, Julius	"		20	"	"	"
729	Bodecker, Otto	"		20	"	"	"
728	Bruns, Herman	"		20	"	"	"
706	Bechtel, Solomon	"	H	59	"	"	"
697	Breslin, Dennis	"		59	"	"	"
695	Blaurett, Geo.	"		59	"	"	"
689	Burns, Thomas	"	B	59	"	"	"

NEW YORK—CONTINUED.

Hendst's No.	NAME.	Rank.	Company	Regim't.	Arm of Service.	Date of Death.	REMARKS.
673	Bordin, William	Private,	G	2	Infantry,	Unknown,	Removed from Antietam battlefield.
645	Blake, J. H.	"	B	21	"	"	" " " "
623	Barrett, John	"	G	78	"	"	" " " "
524	Beardslee, John	"	F	34	"	"	" " " "
565	Burger, Charles	"	C	27	"	Sept. 17, 1862	
585	Baker, Harris	"	"	78	"	Unknown,	
586	Brommer, Andrew	"	I	102	"	Sept. 27, 1862	Smoketown, Md.
618	Bradley, Timothy W.	"	H	22	"	Oct. 4, 1862	Died at South Mountain of typhoid fever.
501	Bacon, John	"	K	59	"	Oct. 31, 1862	Smoketown, Md.
422	Bushnell, David	"	L	121	"	Oct. 18, 1862	Burkettsville, Md.
421	Bissell, Henry	"		16	"	Oct. 8, 1862	"
398	Brown, Amos	"	A	5	Cavalry,	July 25, 1864	Harper's Ferry.
284	B——, H——	"	C			Unknown,	Weverton,
286	Birdsall, Albert I.	"	G	5	Heavy Artill'y,	Nov. 2, 1864	Died at Knoxville, Md, of disease.
314	Bogart, Henry L.	"	K	89	Infantry,	Nov. 3, 1862	Weverton.
324	Binson, Edward	"	K	78	"	Oct. 13, 1864	"
328	Brand, David J.	"	K	44	"	Oct. 5, 1862	
334	Brink, Elias	Corporal,	B	137	"	Oct. 4, 1864	Age 37—Weverton.
341	Burns, ——	Private,				Unknown,	Weverton.
360	Betson, Thomas	"	E	32	"	Nov. 27, 1862	Burkettsville.
374	Barnes, William H.	"	F	49	"	Nov. 10, 1862	At Hagerstown, Md.
270	Bugbee, Henry F.	3d Serg't,	K	51	"	Oct. 20, 1862	Frederick.
242	Britton, Edward	Private,	E	69	"	Oct. 28, 1862	"
230	Burger, Edward T.	"	H	64	"	Nov. 17, 1862	
215	Bray, George	"	A	69	"	Dec. 2, 1862	
769	Beaver, William	"	K	75	"	Sept. 17, 1862	Antietam battlefield.
375	Boyle, Thomas	1st Serg't,	H	33	"	Nov. 16, 1862	Hagerstown, Md.
195	Barons, Henry	Private,		108	"	Dec. 22, 1862	Removed from Frederick.
189	Bradford, James	"	D	4	"	Feb. 4, 1863	Removed from Frederick—Age 25.
187	Boyle, Bryan	"		145	"	Jan. 24, 1863	Removed from Frederick.
174	Brunson, W. F.	"	I		Cavalry,	July 23, 1863	Removed from Frederick—Age 23.

DESCRIPTIVE LIST. 65

No.	Name	Rank	Co.	Regt.	Arm	Date		Remarks
61	Burns, M. O.	Private,	A	15	Cavalry,	July	9, 1864	Removed from Frederick.
70	Black, Oscar D.	"	K	9	Heavy Artil'y,	July	12, 1864	Killed at Monocacy.
102	Boneling, Thomas	"	C	106	Infantry,	Aug.	11, 1864	Died of wounds received in action.
107	Barrett, J. F.	"	K	75	"	Sept.	18, 1864	Removed from Frederick.
118	Butcher, John	"	B	75	"	Oct.	12, 1861	
131	Bradburn, P. W.	"	H	9	Heavy Artil'y,	Feb.	8, 1865	
140	Bigelow, Anson D.	Corporal,	E	60	Infantry,	Oct.	2, 1862	
141	Burer, John, or John O'Brien.	Sergeant,	D	66	"	Oct.	2, 1862	May be Adolphe Bader of Company D.
145	Baden, Augustus	Private,		7	"	Sept.	4, 1862	Removed from Frederick.
151	Burke, Waller	"	I	69	"	Sept.	27, 1862	Died at Cumberland Gap, Md.
38	Branch, Oscar B.	"	H	106	"	Sept.	26, 1862	Removed from Frederick.
29	Baulton, William	"	D	21	Cavalry,	July	16, 1864	
14	Butler, John	"	C	21	"	May	3, 1865	
12	Bloom, Henry E.	"	F	15	"	June	15, 1864	
11	Reymier, Frederick	"	L	1	"	Sept.	16, 1863	
69	Burke, Simeon	"	H	21	Infantry,	July	15, 1864	Frederick, Md.
741	Carmichael, Alfred	Sergeant,	I	9	"			Antietam battlefield.
750	Collins, Levi	Private,		51	"			
776	Chamberlain, Myron	"	E	51	"			May be Thomas Curley.
779	Connerty, Thomas	"	F	89	U. S. S. S.	Sept.	29, 1862	Died of wounds. Received at Antietam.
824	Courtney, Charles J.	"		2	Infantry,			" "
837	Coffin, H. F.	"		20	"			" "
842	Coffee, Michael	"		42	"			" "
712	Connors, Thomas	"		87	"			" "
704	Corstirupplcicutt, Wenepetheous	"		2	"			" "
681	Corpers, P.	"		21	"			" "
648	Curran, T. A.	"	G	21	"			" "
644	Carson, Mathew	"	D	107	"	Sept.	17, 1862	" "
634	Callahan, Patrick	"	I	59	"			" "
541	Craig, F.	"		1	Battery,			" "
542	Chambers, R.	"	A	104	Infantry,	Oct.	2, 1862	" "
551	Crawford, Charles N.	"	K	108	"			Antietam battlefield, color bearer.
553	Casey, Miles	"	L	27	"			Died of wounds received at Antietam.
566	Coller, Thomas	"	C	104	"	July	20, 1863	Died of wounds, Gettysburg, July 1, 1863.
571	Catlin, David M.	"	H	22	"	Oct.	11, 1862	Died of wounds, Antietam battlefield.
595	Campbell, Edward	"	K	59	"	Nov.	12, 1862	Smoketown, Md.
605	Carr, John	"	D	104	"	Nov.	12, 1862	"
609	Christy, Andrew							

ANTIETAM NATIONAL CEMETERY.

NEW YORK—CONTINUED.

Headst'e No.	NAME	Rank	Company	Regim't	Arm of Service	Date of Death	REMARKS
613	Crawford, Walter	Private,	E	27	Infantry,	Feb. 27, 1865	Died at hospital, chronic diarrhœa.
621	Cleveland, Peter H.	"	L	97	"	Oct. 23, 1862	Smoketown.
504	Cook, Allen C.	"	E	105	"	Oct. 24, 1862	
485	Clark, Alvin	"	G	24	"	Aug. 30, 1862	Killed in action, South Mountain.
472	Coon, Joseph L.	Corporal,	B	76	"	Sept. 14, 1862	South Mountain.
471	Coates, George	Private,		28	"		"
461	Clarke, George E.	"		66	"		"
458	Conklin, W. H.	"	A	14	S. M.		Removed from Middletown.
456	Curry, James E.	"	E	84	Infantry,	Sept. 30, 1862	Wounded at Antietam, died at Middletown.
431	Collins, Enos S.	"	B	16	"	Sept. 29, 1862	" " "
426	Campbell, John	"	E	33	"	April 17, 1864	Died at Burkettsville, Md.
408	Cowan, John	"	B	5	"		" " "
289	C. C.						" " "
310	Chevalere, Edwin	Corporal,	A	5	Heavy Art'y,		Died at Weverton.
318	Cronk, Henry	Private,	F	5	"		"
327	Cayler, Leonard	"	H	10	Infantry,		"
354	Cole, William	"	E	15	Cavalry,	Aug. 29, 1864	Died at Burkettsville.
356	Cunningham, G. N.	"	A	16	Infantry		"
361	Casler, Joseph	"	H	121	"	Nov. 12, 1862	Died at Hagerstown.
383	Conklin, H. S.	"	E	3	"	Nov. 16, 1862	Removed from Hagerstown.
384	Campbell, John W.	"	G	49	"	Nov. 24, 1862	Died at Hagerstown.
390	Carpenter, Cyrus	"	B	121	"	Oct. 24, 1862	" "
254	Corrigan, John	"	D	107	"	Oct. 24, 1862	Died of wounds received at Antietam.
244	Callighan, Patrick	Sergeant,	B	69	"	Oct. 28, 1862	Died at Frederick.
238	Curly, John	Private,	E	137	"	Nov. 7, 1862	"
226	Cram, James	"	L	9	S. M.	Nov. 3, 1862	"
217	Cross, Charles J.	"	G	124	Infantry,	July 14, 1863	Age 22 – Died at Frederick.
185	Conklin, John H. H.	"	E	15	Cavalry,	June 3, 1864	Died at Frederick.
169	Conklin, John	"	C	9	Heavy Art'y,	July 13, 1864	"
64	Carroll, James	"	H	106	Infantry,	July 17, 1864	"
77	Conger, William H. H.	"					

DESCRIPTIVE LIST.   67

		Rank	Co.	No.	Arm	Date		Year	Remarks
79	Casselman, Albert	Private,	K	9	Heavy Artl'y,	July	9,	1864	Killed at Monocacy.
93	Copp, Joseph	"	H	15	Infantry,	July	23,	1864	Removed from Frederick.
100	Cole, Charles S.	"	K	75	"	Aug.	17,	1864	Removed from Frederick.
105	Crawford, M. H.	Sergeant,	A	72	"	Aug.	24,	1864	Removed from Frederick.
117	Carpenter, Albert H.	Private,	B	156	"	Oct.	27,	1864	Removed from Frederick.
124	Conmerford, Daniel	"	C	69	"	Sept.	20,	1862	Removed from Frederick.
126	Curry, John	"		5	Heavy Artl'y,	Jan.	16,	1865	Removed from Frederick.
134	Cormick, John	"	B	9	Cavalry,	April	5,	1862	Removed from Frederick.
157	Clum, Chauncey J.	"	H	33	Infantry,	Oct.	1,	1862	Wounded at Antietam, Sept. 17, 1862, died at [Frederick, Md.
163	Cullen, Frank	"	M	24	"	Oct.	5,	1862	Died at Frederick.
46	Curry, Joseph	Corporal,	E	15	Cavalry,				Died at Frederick.
44	Carty, M.	Private,	E	1	"				Died at Frederick.
34	Cheney, James A.	"		106	Infantry,	Dec.	13,	1862	Cumberland Gap.
1	Cook, P. E.	"		89	"	Unknown,			Removed from Antietam battlefield.
28	Cook, Walter	"	K	15	Cavalry,	Nov.	11,	1864	Removed from Clarysville.
18	Clements, Aaron	"	H	1	"	Oct.	7,	1864	Removed from Clarysville.
5	Clafferty, P. M.	Corporal,		51	Infantry,				Removed from Antietam battlefield.
4	Conway, James	Private,		9	"				Removed from Antietam battlefield.
180	Davis, Miles	"	H	89	"	Mar.	8,	1863	Frederick, Md.
742	Delavergue, G. A.	"		9	"				Antietam battlefield.
755	Devlin, John	"	H	9	"				Antietam battlefield.
759	Donohoe, Francis	"	G	9	"				May be Thomas, Antietam battlefield.
778	Dall, Robert C.	"	A	51	"				Removed from Antietam battlefield.
832	Donohoe, James	"	E	34	"	Sept.	17,	1852	Removed from Antietam battlefield
835	Dobbins, Thomas	"	G	42	"				Removed from Antietam battlefield
734	Dutton, Jonathan R.	"	A	49	"	Sept.	17,	1862	Killed in action Antietam.
714	Duffy, John	"		42	"				Antietam battlefield.
711	Darcey, Patrick	"		42	"				May be Bernard Dearry, Antietam battlefield.
690	Davidson, Samue	"	B	59	"				Antietam battlefield.
686	Davis, John C.	"		26	"				Antietam battlefield.
683	Donoley, Michael	"		105	"				Antietam battlefield.
550	Dudman, Charles	"	B	7	"				Antietam battlefield.
477	Dose, ——	"							South Mountain.
427	Davis, Wm.	"	C	121	Artillery	Dec.	9,	1862	Died at Burkettsville, Md.
399	Donelson, Walter	"	L						Died at Weverton.
397	Dunham, John R.	"	R	24	Cavalry,	July	30,	1864	Died at Weverton.
396	D——, David	"							Died at Weverton.
309	Dorlan, George	"	F	10	Infantry.				Died at Weverton.

NEW YORK—CONTINUED.

Hendst'e No.	NAME.	Rank.	Company	Regt'ne	Arm of Service.	Date of Death.		REMARKS.
319	Denfetney, James	Private,	B	77	Infantry,	Aug. 4,	1864	Died at Weverton.
365	Delano, Macey	"	E	108	"	Nov. 20,	1862	Died at Hagerstown,
255	Dooling, Patrick (or Dolan)	"	K	11	"	Oct. 10,	1862	"
229	Dows, James G.	"	I	77	"	Nov. 25,	1862	"
225	Donley, Edward	"	C	55	"	Nov. 7,	1862	"
222	Dudeck, Alexander	"	B	7	"	Nov. 3,	1862	"
211	Diendonnie, M.	"	E	1	Infantry, L. I.,	Nov. 24,	1862	"
197	Darragh, John	"	D	145	"	Dec. 20,	1862	"
194	Delaney, John	"	C	57	"	Dec. 26,	1862	[Hagerstown.
172	Dunn, M. H.	Corporal,	H	168	"	Aug. 30,	1863	Age 18—May be Myron H. Dean. Died at
272	Dean, Patrick							Antietam battlefield.
268	Dix, Hosea		H	15	Cavalry,	Oct. 18,	1862	Frederick. Md.
60	Decker, George	Private,	L	59	Infantry,	July 9,	1864	Died at Hagerstown.
144	Dooling, Patrick	"	I	107	"	Oct. 3,	1862	"
150	Dawson, Mathew S.	"	H	63	"	Sept. 27,	1862	Died at Frederick.
52	Daley, Timothy	Sergeant,	A	15	"	Oct. 9,	1862	Died at Fred'k. of wounds rec'd at Antietam.*
26	Dolson, Frank	Private,		192	"	May 15,	1864	Removed from Clarysville.*
16	Davis, William F.	"	D	51	"	April 21,	1865	Died at Cumberland.*
780	Eichendure, A.	"	C	59	"			May be Albert Eckenacus.*
694	Erskine, Theodore	"	G	26	"			May be Charles W.*
687	Evans, William							
668	Eagon, James	Corporal,	G	42	"			
537	Eister, Louis	Private,	D	4	"	Nov. 30,	1862	Smoketown, Md.
503	Elliott John	"	C	21	"	Sept. 17,	1862	Killed in action at Antietam.
498	Ebert, Augustus	"	F	130	"	Sept. 14,	1862	Killed in action at South Mountain.
489	Evans, James	Sergeant,	K	22	Cavalry,	Oct. 7,	1864	Weverton.
298	Eldridge, Milo D.	Private,	L	22	"	Sept. 22,	1864	Age 54 years—Weverton.
312	Ellsworth, Orison	"	A	9	Infantry,	Oct. 13,	1862	Removed from Frederick.
264	Emery, Frederick V.	"	E	14	"	Oct. 24,	1862	Removed from Frederick.
243	Emrich, Henry	"	B	20				

*Removed from Antietam battlefield.

DESCRIPTIVE LIST.

No.	Name	Rank	Co.	Regt.	Branch	Date	Year	Remarks
50	Eyre, Alfred	Private,	E	4	Cavalry,	July 8,	1862	Removed from Frederick.
32	Emly, Thomas	"	G	15	Infantry,	July 12,	1864	Removed from Cumberland.
768	Finns, Dennis	Sergeant,	H	51	"	"		Removed from Antietam battlefield.
789	Francis, Joseph	Private,	C	4	"	"		Removed from Antietam battlefield.
791	Fuller, William	"	C	64	"	"		Removed from Antietam battlefield.
792	Foster, Norman O.	Corporal,	D	64	"	Sept. 17,	1862	Killed in action. Removed from Antietam battlefield.
846	Frey, Frederick	Sergeant,	A	103	"			
678	Foley, Cornelius	Private,	B	2	"	Sept. 19,	1862	Died wounds rec'd Antietam. Rem'd from battlefield.
637	French, John H.	"	A	107	"	Feb. 9,	1863	Died Smoketown. [Antietam battlefield.
591	Floyd, Benjamin	"	B	5	"	Nov. 30,	1862	
620	Fields, Myron H.	"	M	21	"	Nov. 25,	1862	Died at Hagerstown.
388	Fox, Aaron	"	B	32	"	May 22,	1862	"
389	Frost, George	"	G	1	Artillery	Oct. 12,	1862	Wounded at Antietam, died at Frederick.
262	Fably, Dennis	"	H	66	Infantry,	Nov. 7,	1862	Died at Frederick.
223	Fachndrich, Julius	"	E	103	"	Nov. 29,	1852	"
212	Freeman, Alonzo	"	E	61	"	July 8,	1864	"
73	Floid, J. N.	"	L	15	Cavalry,	July 13,	1864	"
74	Fales, Anthony	"	A	9	Heavy Artl'v,	Aug. 18,	1864	"
101	Flinn, Michael	"	M	21	Cavalry,	Oct. 9,	1862	"
162	Finn, Michael	"	D	88	Infantry,			
42	Fox, William	"	D	15	Cavalry,	Nov. 12,	1864	Died at Cumberland.
30	Foster, Jacob C.	"	H	105	Infantry,	Oct. 1,	1862	Died at Chrysville.
142	Fish, Harry	"	E	4	Cavalry,	July 18,	1862	Died at Frederick.
138	Fisher, Adolphus	"	E	21	"	July 1,	1864	"
65	Fitzroy, Reginald	"	F	4	Infantry,	Oct. 1,	1862	"
152	Furlong, Patrick	"	C	9	"			Removed from Antietam battlefield.
749	Gunther, William	"	E	9	"			May be Franz Gosser, rem'd Antietam battlefield.
753	Groser, Franz	"		9	"			May be Philip Gass, rem'd f'm Antietam battlefield.
754	Glaseer, Philip	"	I	9	"			Removed from Antietam battlefield. [field.
775	Grogen, T. R.	"	B	61	"			"
834	Gallager, Hughey	"	D	7	"			"
816	Graf, John	"		20	"			"
821	Gramlich, Martin	"	A	34	"			"
831	Gilman, Henry	"	F	89	"			"
849	Gray, Richard G.	"		59	"			"
701	Goodnough, Jonathan	"		59	"	Sept. 17,	1862	Died of wounds received at Antietam.
693	Geisler, Francis	Corporal,		2	"	Sept. 22,	1862	Removed from Antietam battlefield.
676	Gilligan, Thomas H.	Private,						"

ANTIETAM NATIONAL CEMETERY.

NEW YORK—CONTINUED.

Head'st'e No.	NAME.	Rank.	Company	Regiment.	Arm of Service.	Date of Death.	REMARKS.
672	Geraty, Martin	Private,	C	2	Infantry,		Removed from Antietam battlefield.
657	Garrity, William	"	E	2	"		"
544	Green, Alonzo	"	F	35	"		"
581	Grissman, Michael	Corporal,	H	9	"		"
587	Grarie, Ferdinand	Private,	E	42	"	Oct. 10, 1862	Died at Smoketown.
612	Goodall, Asaph	"	A	33	"	Feb. 10, 1863	Died at Smoketown hospital.
497	Gilvoy, James	"		103	"		Smoketown.
495	Gestbent, Nicholas	"		103	"		Antietam battlefield.
455	Gillen, James S.	Sergeant,	F	21	Cavalry,		"
287	Gordon, Samuel	Private,		3	Artillery,	Aug. 4, 1864	Middletown.
348	Glass, John	"	H	20	Infantry,	Nov. 20, 1862	Weverton.
387	Gentz, Christian	"			"	Oct. 19, 1862	Hagerstown.
278	Golder, Joseph	"	F	8	"	Nov. 21, 1862	Died at Frederick. Removed from Frederick.
228	Griffis, Hoy O.	"	F	49	"	Nov. 15, 1862	Removed from Frederick.
227	Giggly, Rudolph	"	B	51	"	Nov. 4, 1862	"
218	Gandal, George	Corporal,	F	18	"	Dec. 11, 1862	Died of wounds at Fred'k. Rem'd f'm An-
214	Goodrich, Allen	Private,	I	97	"	Dec. 7, 1862	Removed from Frederick. [tietam battlefield.
204	Gibbs, William	"	G	69	"	Dec. 24, 1862	Removed from Frederick.
198	Gitney, Thomas	"	F	151	"	Aug. 4, 1864	Removed from Frederick.
81	Green, T. W.	"	D	35	"	Sept. 26, 1862	Died at Frederick. Removed from Frederick.
130	Geinor, Frederick	"	D	97	"	Oct. 2, 1862	May be Anson James, of Co. C. Rem'd from
155	Gavey, Anson	"	D	12	"	Oct. 20, 1862	Rem'd from Antietam battlefield. [Fred'rick.
740	Howard, David H.	Sergeant,	G	9	"		May be Thomas H. Rem'd f'm Antietam
752	Holland, Patrick	Private,	H	51	"		Rem'd f'm Antietam battl-field. [battlefield.
783	Higgins, James	"	B	108	"		Removed from Antietam battlefield.
813	Hammel, Bernard	"	C	79	"	Sept. 17, 1862	Killed in action. Rem'd f'm Antietam battle-
848	Harris, George	Corporal,	I	77	"		Removed from Antietam battlefield. [field.
722	Huntington, George	Sergeant,		42	"		Removed from Antietam battlefield.
717	Henry, Robert	Private,	C	42	"		Removed from Antietam battlefield.
713	Hawksby, George	"		76	"		Antietam battlefield.
460	Howell, Tappan						

DESCRIPTIVE LIST. 71

No.	Name	Rank	Co.	Regiment	Date	Year	Remarks
670	Howe, Nicholas	Private,	B	6 Battery,			Removed from Antietam battlefield.
664	Hacker, Charles E.	"		2 Infantry,			"
661	Hanman, Patrick	"	F	59 "			"
655	Hawkey, George	"		2 "			"
567	Hickman, George W.	"	C	14 "	Oct. 12,	1862	May be Jacob Hickman. Rem'd f'm Antietam [battlefield.
583	Hair, Daniel B.	"	C	16 "	Nov. 13,	1862	Near Bakersville, Md.
606	Hays, Raswell F.	"	E	35 "	Nov. 11,	1862	Smoketown.
614	Hascall, Arthur Foot	Sergeant,	G	61 "			"
506	Hathaway, Charles	Private,	A	23 "	Nov. 28,	1862	Died of wounds at Antietam. Smoketown.
488	Harris, James	"	I	94 "			South Mountain.
463	Holtz, A.	"		85 "			"
441	Harnot, Julius	"	A	16 "			Middletown.
439	Howley, Edmund B.	"	C	18 "	Sept. 14,	1862	Killed at Crampton's Pass, Md, S. Mountain.
429	Heythorn, Maurice E.	"		18 "			Burkettsville.
414	Heatherton, ——			Heavy Artil'y,			
409	Hall, Albert	"	M	5 "	July 31,	1864	Maryland Heights.
283	Hanlin, James	"	B	195 Infantry,	Aug. 26,	1864	Weverton.
297	Hallan, William	"	A	15 Cavalry,	Feb. 9,	1864	"
304	Hull, Herman D.	Sergeant,	B	15 "			
395	Hoffman, David	Private,	F	Heavy Artil'y,			
329	Hopkins, George	"	L	6 Battery,	Oct. 16,	1864	Age 38—Weverton.
336	Hinman, Wait	"		5 Heavy Artil'y,	July 1,	1864	"
337	Hanton, John	"	G	35 Infantry,			Hagerstown.
344	Hale, George C.	"	A	27 "			"
345	Hoyt, Jesse	"	G	49 "	Dec. 1,	1862	Died at Hagerstown,
377	Haines, Sylvester L.	"	G	121 "	Nov. 21,	1862	"
394	Harrall, William	"	I	63 "	Oct. 16,	1862	Died at Frederick.
271	Horan, Michael B.	"	G	4 "	Nov. 5,	1862	"
221	Hoye, Patrick	"	A	108 "	Dec. 5,	1862	"
206	Herry, Lewis	"	B	145 "	Jan. 5,	1863	"
199	Hemmerich, Christian	"	F	146 "	July 2,	1863	"
183	Hannay, Theron	"	K	41 "	July 15,	1863	Frederick.
176	Holtzman, William	"	H	15 Cavalry,	July 8,	1864	"
62	Hoyt, J. N.	"	M	1 "	July 16,	1864	Died at Frederick.
76	Huges, John	"	K	151 Infantry,	July 16,	1864	"
80	Horsefall, George	"	G	1 "	July 28,	1864	"
92	Haas, Edward	"	M	5 Heavy Artil'y,	July 30,	1864	"
94	Houghtaling, A.						

72   ANTIETAM NATIONAL CEMETERY.

NEW YORK—Continued.

Headst'e No.	Name	Rank	Company	Regiment	Arm of Service	Date of Death	Remarks
96	Hebler, Paul	Private,	H	106	Infantry	July 29, 1864	Died at Frederick.
109	Heeley, Thomas	"	L	2	"	Sept. 9, 1864	Removed from Frederick.
129	Honke, Nathan	"	K	1	Artillery,	July 19, 1862	" " "
53	Hughes, Thomas	"	E	59	Infantry,	Oct. 9, 1862	" " "
43	Hawks, James T.	"	B	15	Cavalry,		Cumberland.
40	Hutchings, George H.	"	B	106	Infantry,	Nov. 13, 1862	Died at Cumberland Gap, Md.
39	Hamblin, Elijah	"	D	106	"	Nov. 23, 1862	" " " "
37	Hobbs, Benjamin	"	I	106	"	Nov. 13, 1863	" " " "
301	Ira, A. I.	"	C	9	"	Unknown,	Frederick, Md.
758	Johnston, David	"	I	9	"		Weverton.
774	Johnson, John F.	"	B	59	"		Antietam battlefield.
698	Judge, Michael	"		21	"		Antietam battlefield.
543	Johnson, C. E.	"	B	31	"		Antietam battlefield.
593	Jolly, Peter	"	D	17	"	Oct. 9, 1862	Antietam battlefield
350	——, W——	"		10	"		Smoketown, Md.
235	Johnson, Phineas E.	Sergeant,	F	151	"	Nov. 20, 1862	May be Wm. Jones, Co. D. and E. Antietam.
85	Johnson, E. W.	Private,	A	9	Heavy Art'y,	Aug. 20, 1864	Removed from Frederick.
88	Johnson, Horace H.	"	D	5	"	July 28, 1864	Removed from Frederick.
99	Jackson, Henry	"	B	15	Infantry,	Aug. 4, 1864	Died at Frederick.
114	Johnson, John	"	C	2	"	Oct. 16, 1864	Died at Frederick, of wounds at Monocacy.
154	Jameson, John E.	"	K	6	Cavalry,	Oct. 3, 1862	Frederick, Md.
19	Jones, William H.	"		106	Infantry,	May 11, 1865	"
35	Jarvis, Alfred	Corporal,	I	51	"	Unknown,	Clarysville.
786	Keefe, Michael	Private,	F	66	"		Antietam battlefield.
808	Keenan, Patrick	"	F	66	"		Antietam battlefield.
809	Kane, William	"	B	20	"		Antietam battlefield.
823	Kaufman, John	"	A	20	"		Antietam battlefield.
839	Kayser, Jacob	"		20	"		Antietam battlefield.
841	Kurtz, Jacob	"		20	"		Antietam battlefield.
731	Kensing, Charles	"		59	"		Antietam battlefield.
702	Kennie, J. D.	"			"		Antietem battlefield.

DESCRIPTIVE LIST.

No.	Name	Rank	Co.	Regiment	Date	Year	Remarks
682	Kelley, Jeremiah	Private,		2 Infantry,	Sept. 22,	1862	Antietam battlefield.
666	Klein, Adam	"		2 "	Oct. 10,	1862	Smoketown.
663	Kelly, James	"		2 "	Sept. 14,	1862	Killed at South Mountain, Md.
630	Kelly, John	"		2 "			Middletown.
570	Kidder, Ellis	"	H	4 "			Weverton.
598	Knapp, Benjamin P.	"	K	77 "			
470	Knight, Christopher L.	"		89 "			
452	Kingston, Judkins	"		1 Battery,	Aug. 29,	1864	Age 30. Died at Sandy Hook, Md.
294	King, Cyrel	"	D	160 Infantry,			Weverton.
299	Kelly, Shelden	"	E	5 Heavy Artl'y,			Weverton.
306	Koch, Lewis	"	L	49 Infantry,	Sept. 16,	1862	Hagerstown.
347	Kline, William	"	B	20 "			
349	Kelsh, Jacob	"	K	1 Long Island,	Sept. 20,	1862	
376	Kane, Andrew	Corporal,	H	20 Infantry,	Oct. 21,	1862	Age 23. Hagerstown.
277	Klein, Constantine	Private,	F	63 "	Oct. 20,	1862	Frederick.
248	Keefe, John O.	Sergeant,	C	69 "	Oct. 26,	1862	Died at Frederick.
239	Keilt, John	Private,	B	137 "	Nov. 23,	1862	
201	Kells, James	"	I	9 " S. M.	Jan. 20,	1863	
191	Kenney, Peter B.	"	B	111 "	Aug. 2,	1863	Age 34. Frederick
171	Kimpland, Charles B.	"	E	9 Heavy Artil'y,	July 21,	1864	Died at Frederick.
89	Kirby, Patrick E.	"	I	176 Infantry,	Dec. 21,	1864	"
123	Kitchen, Stephen	"	K	9 "	Oct. 2,	1862	"
160	Kingsland, J. W.	"	H	97 "	Oct. 7,	1862	"
166	Kronmuller, Philip	"	C	8 "	Jan. 29,	1862	"
51	Kaiser, Charles	"	F	89 "	Sept. 17,	1852	Killed in action Antietam.
738	Lewis, Ennis	"		9 "			"
744	Lawrence, Samuel B.	"		9 "			"
787	Lockwood, J. C. F.	Corporal,	C	51 "			Removed from Antietam battlefield.
788	Loud, George W.	Private,		20 "			May be Peter Lenz, Co. H. "
822	Leach, Peter	"		34 "			Removed from Antietam battlefield.
844	Lewis, W. H.	"		20 "			
720	Lichtenheld, Edward	"		42 "			
716	Lee, William						
709	Lane, Stanton	Sergeant,	I	59 "	Sept. 17,	1862	Killed at Antietam. Removed from battlefield.
696	Leach, J. R.	Private,	K	104 "			Removed from Antietam battlefield.
642	Lyons, John	"	A	2 U. S. S. S.	Sept. 20,	1862	Wounded Antietam. Rem'd from battlefield.
594	Livingston, Alexander	"			Nov. 25,	1862	Smoketown.
600	Levick, Casper	"	B	49 Infantry,	Jan. 16,	1863	

ANTIETAM NATIONAL CEMETERY.

NEW YORK—CONTINUED.

Head-st'e No.	NAME	Rank	Company	Reg't line	Arm of Service	Date of Death			REMARKS
502	Lynch, Patrick	Private	E	108	Infantry	Oct.	18,	1862	Smoketown.
486	Lacky, Oliver L.	"	B	22	"	Sept.	14,	1862	Killed at South Mountain.
424	Lapine, Matthew	"		16	"				South Mountain.
423	Lee, Andrew J.	Sergeant	D	16	"	Sept.	15,	1862	Burkettsville, Md.
291	Liebengut, Gottlieb	Corporal	D	4	Cavalry	Sept.	8,	1864	Age 31—Weverton.
313	Lampman, Augustus	Private	B	5	Artillery				Weverton.
331	Lone, Thomas	"	K	89	Infantry	Nov.	14,	1862	Died of disease, Weverton.
346	Lavers, Richard	"	E	27	"				Weverton.
372	Leonard, William N.	"	K	106	"	July	4,	1863	Age 30—Died at Hagerstown.
391	Leach, William	"	D	16	"	Nov.	23,	1862	Died at Hagerstown.
276	Long, August	"	D	20	"	Oct.	21,	1862	Age 18—Died at Hagerstown. Rem'd f'm Fred'k.
253	Leyden, Michael	"	K	63	"	Oct.	23,	1862	Died of wounds Antietam. Rem'd f'm Fred'k.
205	Libby, John	"	D	69	"	Dec.	14,	1862	May be Michael J. Lilly. Rem'd f'm Fred'k.
202	Lebkuchler, Ferd.	"	D	7	"	Dec.	6,	1862	Wounded Antietam. Died at & rem'd f'm Fred'k.
192	Limbark, Jacob	"	D	49	"	Jan.	13,	1863	Died at Frederick. Removed from Frederick.
178	Lang, Joseph	"	G	106	"	May	5,	1863	Age 19—Removed from Frederick.
87	Livermore, Henry W.	"	G	106	"	July	26,	1864	Died at Frederick. Removed from Frederick.
45	Lamphear, Elie	"	A	193	"	Oct.		1865	Cumberland Gap, Md.
22	Ladd, Albert	"	D	15	Cavalry	May	24,	1864	Clarysville.
13	Lindsley, Abraham S.	"	E	15	"	Sept.	15,	1864	"
763	Miles, Lyman S.	Sergeant	K	89	Infantry	Sept.	17,	1862	Killed in battle Antietam.
772	Murg, Joseph	Private	B	103	"	Oct.	2,	1862	"
777	Miller, James H.	"	C	51	"				Antietam battlefield.
782	Miller, Edward	Corporal		51	"				Antietam battlefield.
810	McKibbins, Thomas	Private	F	108	"				Antietam battlefield.
815	Monroe, James L.	"	B	108	"				Antietam battlefield.
735	Meurer, Joseph	"		77	"				Antietam battlefield.
730	Mann, Albert	"	B	20	"				Antietam battlefield.
707	Miller, Samuel	"		59	"				Antietam battlefield.
699	Managan, W.	"		59	"				Antietam battlefield.
691	McMahan, Patrick	"	G	59	"				Antietam battlefield.

DESCRIPTIVE LIST.

688	Morhead, Robert	Private,	L	59	Infantry,		Antietam battlefield.
679	McLauchlin, Patrick	"	"	2	"		"
677	McCorkle, J. H.	"	"	2	"		"
675	Montgomery, F.	"	"	2	"		"
667	Metzinger, Charles	"	"	2	"		"
656	Montgomery, Thomas	"	H	9	S. M.		May be James Morton. Antietam battlefield.
635	Murphy, James	"	"	107	Infantry,	Sept. 13, 1862	Died at Harper's Ferry. Antietam battlefield.
633	Mathews, Charles	"	"	104	"		Antietam battlefield.
539	Massy, Alex.	"	"	20	"		May be George. Antietam battlefield.
547	Mackaboy, E.	"	C	108	"		Antietam battlefield.
561	McKenzie, John	"	K	102	"	Sept. 21, 1862	Killed in action.
601	McGee, Robert	"	E	82	"	Nov. 10, 1862	Smoketown, Md.
603	Moore, Richard	"	C	76	"	Nov. 14, 1862	
607	Mix, Joel	"	E	2	"	Sept. 28, 1862	Antietam battlefield.
494	McKinney, W. M.	"	F	35	"	Sept. 14, 1862	Killed at South Mountain
473	Merritt, Richard D.	"	D	89	"	Sept. 15, 1862	
468	Morse, U. E.	"	G	5	Heavy Art'y,	April 15, 1864	Burkettsville.
405	McGlinchy, John	"	L	5	"	Aug. 13, 1864	Age 21—Sandy Hook.
403	Meyers, Charles	"	L	5	"	July 27, 1864	Sandy Hook, Md.
400	Meyres, Antonio D.	"	L	15	Cavalry,	Sept. 17, 1864	Weverton.
288	Murray, James	"	A	173	Infantry,	Oct. 7, 1864	Harper's Ferry. Removed from Weverton.
311	McCarty, John	"	F	5	Heavy Artil'y,		Removed from Weverton.
316	McCarthy, Jeremiah	"	L	16	Cavalry,	Sept. 12, 1864	"
321	Mott, Charles	"	H	10	Artillery,	Oct. 18, 1864	"
322	Maining, Edward C.	"	B	43	Infantry,	Jan. , 1863	"
326	Maguire, John	"	G	3	Cavalry,	Aug. 2, 1864	
330	Messic, Levi S.	"	B	13	Infantry,	Nov. 4, 1862	Hagerstown.
366	Merrill, G. C.	"	L	77	"	Oct. 19, 1862	
280	Mushgrove, Thomas	"	C	33	"	Nov. 1, 1862	Died in Hospital, at Hagerstown.
279	Murphy, Thomas	"	G	61	"	Oct. 18, 1862	Removed from Frederick.
273	McMahon, John	"	A	61	"	Oct. 16, 1862	"
267	McCoy, John	"	K	69	"	Oct. 18, 1862	"
266	McQueen, James	"	"	46	"	Oct. 21, 1862	"
251	Mullen Emile	"	A	20	"	Oct. 22, 1862	"
245	Mass, Jacob	Corporal,	I	69	"	Oct. 30, 1862	"
240	Magnet, Edward	Sergeant,	E	97	"	Oct. 27, 1862	Died at Frederick.
237	Maxfield, David F.	"	A	145	"	Oct. 24, 1862	"
236	Miller, Daniel P.						

76 ANTIETAM NATIONAL CEMETERY.

NEW YORK—CONTINUED.

Headst'e No.	NAME.	Rank.	Company	Regim't	Arm of Service.	Date of Death.		REMARKS.
736	Miles, T. J.	Private,	I	49	Infantry,	Unknown,		Antietam battlefield.
650	Meckbach, George	"	F	20	"	"		"
231	Miller, John	"	F	18	"	Nov. 17,	1862	Died at Frederick of wounds.
224	Moran, John	"	F	63	"	Nov. 6,	1862	Died at Frederick.
210	McVety, William	"	F	108	"	Dec. 13,	1862	"
203	Madden, William	"	A	61	"	Dec. 7,	1862	"
173	Mason, W. H.	"	A	151	"	July 23,	1863	Age 23.
78	Miller, Alexander	"	A	106	"	July 16,	1864	Died at Frederick.
36	Mann, George	"	K	9	Heavy Artil'y,	July 27,	1864	"
95	McGuire, Hugh	"	F	162	Infantry,	Aug. 5,	1864	"
108	McGill, William	"	H	5	Heavy Artil'y,	Aug. 29,	1864	"
111	Maddrell, James	"	D	2	Cavalry,	Sept. 18,	1864	"
116	Moore, Francis	"	H	—	"	Nov. 22,	1864	"
128	McCarty, Timothy	"	L	60	Infantry,	Aug. 24,	1862	
139	McQuade, Thomas	"	B	69	"	Sept. 24,	1862	
153	McCormic, Patrick	"	C	4	"	Sept. 30,	1862	Removed from Frederick.
156	Murray, Michael	"	B	69	"	Sept. 30,	1862	Removed from Frederick.
158	Morley, John	"	C	6	"	Sept. 28,	1862	Removed from Frederick.
159	Mibbon, Daniel	"	G	13	"	Oct. 3,	1862	Removed from Frederick.
161	Maloney, Thomas	"	K	63	"	Oct. 5,	1862	Wounded at Antietam, died at Frederick.
164	McIlvane, William	"	G	35	"	Oct. 7,	1862	
165	Miller, Edward F.	1st Serg't,	H	99	"	Oct. 7,	1864	
48	Mapes, Seymour B.	Corporal,	D	102	"	July 16,	1862	Died at Frederick.
36	Marsh, Benson B.	Private,	E	106	"	Dec. 8,	1862	Cumberland Gap.
17	Murphy, Michael	"	G	1	Cavalry,	Oct. 26,	1864	Clarysville.
10	Mead, Edward	"	C	3	"	May 25,	1865	Cumberland, Md.
7	Moreland, Alex.	"		51	Infantry,			Antietam battlefield.
745	Negus, Alex.	"	G	9	"			Antietam battlefield
726	Newbury, Lewis	"		20	"			Antietam battlefield
563	Nokes, Martin	"	K	16	"	Oct. 24,	1862	Bakersville, Md.
487	Neason, John	"	G	22	"	Sept. 14,	1862	Killed at South Mountain.

DESCRIPTIVE LIST.

	Name	Rank	Co.	Regiment	Date	Year	Remarks
454	Newton, Thomas K.	Private,	E	89 Infantry,	Sept. 27,	1864	Middletown.
295	Newell, L. D.	"	B	14 Battery;	Oct. 16,	1864	Weverton.
335	Northrop, ——	"	A	"	Oct. 15,	1862	Frederick.
263	Newton, George H.	"	K	105 Infantry,	Oct. 30,	1862	Died of wounds received September 17, 1862.
250	Noble, Harvey	"	E	"	Aug. 8,	1863	Age 24. Frederick
175	Newman, Francis		A	18 "	Oct. 25,	1862	Frederick, Md.
241	Nevin, Thomas		F	63 "	Sept. 2,	1862	Antietam battlefield.
770	O'Connell, John		H	9 "	Sept. 17,	1862	"
825	Orcott, Alvin		E	34 "		1862	"
836	O'Brien, John A.	Sergeant,	C	42 "	Sept. 17,	1862	Killed at Antietam.
534	O'Hara, James	Private,	D	194 "	Aug. 2,	1864	Age 27—Weverton.
325	O'Conner, Dennis	"	K	Cavalry,	Oct. 10,	1862	Hagerstown.
256	O'Brien, Patrick	"	D	2 Infantry,	Nov. 8,	1862	
233	Olds, Orrin W.	"	C	121 "	Feb. 11,	1863	Frederick.
193	O'Neale, Daniel	Sergeant,	K	32 "	Feb. 17,	1862	"
190	O'Brien, James	Private,	F	42 "	Sept. 30,	1862	"
146	O'Neal, Patrick	"	C	88 "	Oct. 4,	1862	"
147	O'Brien, Thomas	"	D	69 "	Oct. 7,	1862	"
148	O'Neale, John	"	I	69 "			
168	O'Reilly, Patrick	"	E	42 "			
751	Patterson, William	Corporal,	D	9 "			Antietam battlefield.
805	Price, James	Private,	K	4 "			May be Edward. Antietam battlefield.
812	Pollay, Samuel B.	"		108 "	Sept. 17,	1862	Antietam battlefield.
719	Propson, Charles	"		20 "			
708	Pritchard, C. B.	"		59 "			
648	Poor, George	"	A	80 "			
653	Pollack, W. J.	"	F	80 "			
652	Pabst, J. P.	Sergeant,		20 "			
647	Price, Thomas P.	Private,		23 "			[tietam battlefield.
646	Ploss, Peter P.	"	E	5 Heavy Artil'y,	Oct. 2,	1862	Died of wounds received at Sharpsburg. An-
538	Parmetier, John H.	"	F	67 Infantry,	Aug. 26,	1864	Weverton.
292	Pittenger, Smith	"	L	"	Nov. 4,	1862	Died at Hagerstown.
363	Patterson, John	"	K	49 "	Oct. 4,	1862	"
364	Price, Chauncey	"	H	66 "	Oct. 11,	1862	Died at Frederick.
261	Paige, James L.	"	M	8 Cavalry,	Nov. 1,	1863	"
249	Page, W. H. H.	"	H	64 Infantry,	Dec. 26,	1862	"
200	Pinner, Samuel	"	H	Indep'nt Bat.	Oct. 12,	1864	
113	Popple, Orville	"					

ANTIETAM NATIONAL CEMETERY.

NEW YORK—Continued.

Headst'e No.	NAME	Rank	Company	Regiment	Arm of Service	Date of Death	REMARKS
122	Putnam, William	Private,	L	116	Infantry,	Nov. 28, 1864	Frederick, Md.
25	Pagefall, Max	"	E	15	Cavalry,	Nov. 3, 1864	Clarysville.
20	Pfeiffer, Augustus	"	K	8	"	"	"
15	Pepper, Nathaniel	"	C	15	"	May 21, 1864	"
784	Quigley, Patrick	"		51	Infantry,	Unknown	Antietam battlefield
764	Rimple, George H.	Corporal,		103	"		Removed from Antietam battlefield
767	Rulapaugh, Nicholas	Private,	C	89	"	Sept. 17, 1862	Killed at Antietam. Removed f'm battlefield.
771	Rasiga, Eugene	"	B	9	"	Sept. 17, 1862	"
773	Raybur, H.	"	H	12	"		Removed from Antietam battlefield. [field.
781	Reynolds, Leander	"		51	"		"
828	Rhoads, Chester S.	"	H	34	"	Sept. 17, 1862	Killed in action. Rem'd f'm Antietam battle-
829	Rubbins, William	"	G	34	"	Sept. 17, 1862	"
733	Renchler, John A.	"	F	77	"		Removed from Antietam battlefield.
721	Ritter, Charles	"		20	"		"
700	Rosegie, S.	"		59	"		"
665	Rehier, Joseph	"	B	2	"		"
651	Riordon, William	"		20	"		" [battlefield.
573	Russ, John M.	"		122	"		" [battlefield.
577	Ringgold, Mathias	Corporal,	I	42	"	Oct. 26, 1862	Died at Downsville. Rem'd from Antietam
582	Reynolds, Stoel F.	Private,	F	51	"		Removed from Antietam battlefield.
584	Robinson, Nelson A.	Corporal,	G	107	"	Nov. 16, 1862	Smoketown.
592	Rogers, William W.	Corporal,	E	105	"	Oct. 11, 1862	Snoketown.
597	Ross, Jacob	Private,	E	22	"	Oct. 14, 1862	Smoketown.
602	Robinson, Rufus	"	I	122	"	Nov. 6, 1862	Smoketown.
443	Rodden, William	"	K	16	"	Sept. 16, 1862	Died of wounds received at Crampton's Gap.
417	Rogers, Amos S.	"	F	107	"	Oct. 7, 1862	Burkettsville, Md.
493	Rehill, Philip	"		2	U. S. Artillery,	Unknown.	Antietam battlefield.
411	Ranerd, C. H.	"		5	Heavy Art'y,		Burkettsville.
410	Rhoda, Frederick	"	M	5	"	Sept. 29, 1864	Maryland Heights.
293	Rice, Charles H.	Sergeant,	E	21	Infantry,		Weverton.
308	Rubinet, James A.	Private,	H	8	Cavalry.		

DESCRIPTIVE LIST.   79

	Name	Rank	Co.	Regt.	Arm	Date		Remarks
315	Rawly, James	Private,	M	4	Cavalry,	Sept. 19,	1864	Weverton.
332	Ryon, Martin	"	A	22	"	Nov. 30,	1864	Sandy Hook, Md.
333	Reese, John	"	K	2	"	Nov. 30,	1854	Age 22—Sandy Hook.
340	Ray, Charles	"		51	Infantry	Oct. 23,	1862	Weverton.
342	Ryan, James	"	K	3	"	Nov. 9,	1862	Hagerstown.
362	Robbins, Sanford	"	A	32	"	Nov. 3,	1862	"
367	Russel, Nathaniel J.	"	C	49	"	Nov. 19,	1862	"
378	Rowley, Simeon E.	"	H	77	"	Nov. 8,	1862	"
382	Rockwell, Daniel	"	K	44	"	Nov. 14,	1862	"
386	Richardson, William	"	A	27	"	Nov. 8,	1862	"
392	Robotham, Thomas	"	C	8	Cavalry,	Nov. 21,	1862	May be Joseph. Hagerstown.
381	Richards, Thomas	"	B	3	Infantry,	Oct. 30,	1862	Died of wounds received at Antietam.
252	Roe, John	"	A	42	"	Oct. 22,	1862	"
246	Robinson, George	"	A	63	"	July 9,	1863	Frederick.
182	Resch, Victor	"	K	40	"	Mar. 30,	1864	"
56	Reed, James	"	H	1	Cavalry,	July 12,	1864	Frederick, Md.
68	Randal, N. S.	"	F	9	Heavy Artil'y,	July 27,	1864	"
90	Rivers, Israel	"	C	106	Infantry,	Sept. 21,	1864	"
110	Rogers, W. H.	"	C	25	"	Nov. 11,	1864	"
115	Reilly, Thomas	"	K	131	"	Oct. 18,	1864	"
120	Riley, Eugene	"	F	131	"	July 5,	1862	"
49	Risdorph, John	Corporal,	F	102	"			
743	Smith, J. A.	Private,		9	"			
756	Shaffer, John	"		9	"			
757	Steveson, W. R.	"		9	"			
766	Schurman, Heinrichs	1st Serg't,	G	103	"	Sept. 17,	1862	Killed in action Antietam. Rem'd f'm battle-field.
761	Stevens, J. J.	Private,		9	"			Removed from Antietam battlefield.
762	Schrey, Christian	Corporal,	F	103	"	Sept. 17,	1862	Killed at Antietam. Rem'd from battlefield.
806	Smith, Joshua	Sergeant,		4	"			Removed from Antietam battlefield
820	Sullivan, John	Corporal,	B	61	"			Removed from Antietam battlefield.
827	Salisbury, William A.	Private,	C	34	Ind't Battery,	Sept. 17,	1862	Killed in action. Rem'd from Antietam.
830	Seuft, Rudolph	"		30	Infantry,	July 27,	1863	Age 57—Removed from Antietam battlefield.
843	Smith, J.			34	"			Removed from Antietam battlefield.
723	Seigfred, Charles P.	Corporal,	A	33,	"	Sept. 17,	1862	Killed. Removed from Antietam battlefield.
710	Stanford, Richard	Private,	D	42	"			May be Stewart Standiford Removed from
680	Shaffer, W.			2	"			Rem'd f'm Antietam battlefield. [Antietam.
671	Simpson, James	"	H	2	"			Removed from Antietam battlefield
649	Springer, C.			73	"			Removed from Antietam battlefield

NEW YORK—Continued.

Head't'e No.	NAME.	Rank.	Company	Reg't	Arm of Service.	Date of Death.	REMARKS.
631	Salmon, S.	Private,	G	1	N. Y. Vols., Artillery,	Sept. 17, 1862	Removed from Antietam battlefield.
629	Salsbury, Reubin E.	"	L	69	Infantry,		Removed from Antietam battlefield.
523	Sauber, J. D.	"		108	"		Removed from Antietam battlefield.
552	Steiner, Rhinehardt	Corporal,	K	49	"		Removed from Antietam battlefield.
564	Sturdivant, Charles	Private,	F	104	"	Sept. 30, 1862	Died at Bakersville. Removed from Antietam.
569	Shepard, L. W.	"	E	9	"	Feb. 13, 1864	Removed from Antietam battlefield.
578	Sweetman, Henry	"	G	103	"		Removed from Antietam battlefield.
580	Schwerin, Herman	"	C	2	"	Oct. 6, 1862	Removed from Antietam battlefield.
589	Smith, Thomas	"	C	60	"		Removed from Smoketown.
599	Severance, Gersham	"	L	104	"	Sept. 23, 1862	Removed from Smoketown.
604	Slack, William	Corporal,	C	76	"	Nov. 8, 1862	Sharpsburg, Md. Removed from Smoketown.
617	Smith, Hezekiah	Private,	D	105	"	Oct. 31, 1862	Removed from Smoketown.
619	Stearns, Sebastian	"	D	97	"	Oct. 7, 1862	Removed from Smoketown.
622	Snyder, William	"	A	105	"	Oct. 26, 1862	Removed from Smoketown.
508	Schults, John	"		76	"	Sept. 14, 1862	Removed from Smoketown.
474	Stamp, Charles E.	"		4	Battery,		South Mountain.
469	Seibert, Josephus	"		95	Infantry,		"
467	Smith, John	"	K	18	"		Middletown.
459	Sickles, Silas	"	C	107	"	Sept. 14, 1862	Killed at Crampton's Pass, Md.
430	Storms, William J.	"	F	46	"	Oct. 12, 1862	Burkettsville, Md
416	Stickler, Gilbert C.	"	G	49	"		Weverton.
290	Schlaich, John	"	C		"	Oct.	Age 19. Weverton.
300	Shriney, Michael	"			"		Weverton.
320	Smith, Stephen B.	"	M	122	Cavalry,	Oct. 9, 1864	Age 34. Weverton.
323	Steinback, Michael	"	K	122	Infantry,	Oct. 29, 1862	Age 24—Hagerstown.
371	Seymour, George B.	"	F		"	Nov. 14, 1862	Hagerstown.
381	Spink, J. M.	"			"	Nov. 30, 1862	Hagerstown.
585	Spicer, Oscar A.	Sergeant,	B	26	"	Oct. 13, 1862	May be Jos. Spoor, Co. G. Died at Frederick.
265	Spiers, Myron	Private,	K	57	"	Oct. 11, 1862	Wounded Antietam. Died at & rem'd Fred'k.
259	Stellwell, Clark	"	K		"		
258	Sherman, Aaron,	"	F	22	"	Oct. 10, 1862	Removed from Frederick.

DESCRIPTIVE LIST.   81

232	Suffolk, Owen	Private,	K	66	Infantry,	Nov. 12, 1862	Removed from Frederick.
216	Stephens, Peter C.	"	H	5	"	Dec. 3, 1862	Died of wounds. Rem'd from Frederick.
213	She, Michael	"	B	61	"	Nov. 25, 1862	Removed from Frederick.
188	Slattery, Patrick	"	C	10	"	Jan. 15, 1863	Age 30. Rem'ed from Fred'k. [I'm Fred'k.
170	Stevens, George E.	"	D	144	"	July 20, 1863	Age 22. May be Milton A. Co. K. Removed
66	Saur, Andrew	"	K	1	Cavalry,	June 27, 1864	Died at Frederick. Removed f'm Frederick.
67	Spiker, J.	"		120	Infantry,	July 12, 1864	Removed from Frederick.
72	Saurs, William	"	C	9	Heavy Artil'y,	July 14, 1864	"
103	Swift, Edward B.	"	E	9	"	Aug. 18, 1864	Died at Frederick. Removed from Frederick.
104	Snow, John	"	L	5	Cavalry,	Sept. 6, 1864	"
106	Spahr, George	"	D	9	Heavy Artil'y,	Aug. 17, 1864	Removed from Frederick.
121	Shuster, Nicholas	"	C	175	Infantry,	Jan. 2, 1865	Died at Frederick. Removed from Frederick.
133	Shenp, John	"			"	Sept. 26, 1862	Removed from Frederick.
135	Schiffoucher, Theodore	"	M	5	Heavy Artil'y,	May 30, 1865	Removed from Antietam battlefield.
840	Sokolosky, Leonarrl	"	B	20	Infantry,	Unknown,	"
727	Shessler, Philip	"	C	20	"		"
746	Seward, W. M.	Corporal,	F	9	"		"
838	Smidt, Charles	Private,					
136	Stephany, Hiram	"	A	32	Indep'nt Bat.	April 3, 1865	Removed from Frederick.
47	Stevenson, James J.	"	I	84	Infantry,	Sept. 24, 1864	"
41	Stiles, George	"	C	106	"	Apr. 4, 1862	Died at Cumberland, Md.
27	Sharat, Daniel	"		54	"		Clarysville.
24	Saol, Louis	"	E	1	Cavalry,	May 4, 1865	"
21	Stringer, Michael	"	C	5	Artillery	Dec. 23, 1864	"
9	Swan, James O.	"	M	25	Cavalry,	May 19, 1865	Died at Cumberland, Md.
739	Taylor, Henry H.	"	I	6	"	Sept. 30, 1862	Antietam.
785	Thompson, John	"	B	51	Infantry,		"
705	Terry, G. W.	"	C	59	"		May be Charles W. Taylor. Antietam.
703	Thomas, Horace	"		59	"		Antietam.
560	Tillotsen, Charles A.	"	G	108	"		"
596	Tice, Charles W.	"	F	23	"	Oct. 5, 1862	Smoketown.
615	Tnafe, Edward	"		42	"	Oct. 7, 1862	Middletown.
453	Turner, J. H.	"					
451	Tracy, Michael	"		9	"		
444	T——, J.	"					
282	Tyneson, Daniel F.	"	I	4	Cavalry,	Aug. 8, 1864	Weverton.
343	Taylor, Washington L.	"	I	43	Infantry,		Hagerstown.
234	Teller, Pierre	"	K	88	"	Nov. 8, 1862	Frederick.

ANTIETAM NATIONAL CEMETERY.

NEW YORK—CONTINUED.

Headst'e No.	NAME.	Rank.	Company	Reg'ment	Arm of Service.	Date of Death.	REMARKS.
219	Trainor, Patrick	Private,	C	42	Infantry,	Nov. 5, 1862	Frederick.
112	Timmerson, Oscar	"	C	9	Heavy Artil'y,	Nov. 11, 1864	"
127	Tyron, William B.	"	D	1	Cavalry,	Mar. 3, 1865	"
54	Turner, P. H.	"	D	2	Infantry,	Oct. 8, 1862	"
23	Taylor, Eldridge F.	"	L	21	Cavalry,	Oct. 4, 1864	Died at Cumberland, Md.
8	Tripp, William B.	"	D	15	"	Sept. 2, 1864	Clarysville.
179	Tripp, Charles W.	"	F	146	Infantry	July 8, 1863	Age 26. Frederick
260	Tucker, Frank	Corporal,	G	14	"	Oct. 13, 1863	Removed from Frederick.
91	Tierney, Daniel	Private,	C	21	"	July 23, 1864	"
737	Van Antwerp, Adelbert A. J.	Corporal,	A	89	"	Sept. 17, 1862	Killed in action. Antietam.
847	Van Cott, David	Private,	E	9	"		Antietam battlefield.
522	Vandevere, William B.	"	E	59	"		"
407	Van Tassel, Isaac	Corporal,	A	6	"	Feb. 6, 1863	Burkettsville, Md
209	Vinton, Everill C.	Private,	F	108	"	Dec. 9, 1862	Frederick.
132	Van Sickles, Seymour	"	K	78	"	Sept. 10, 1862	"
143	Vater, Charles	"	A	7	"	Sept. 30, 1862	"
428	Van Arnum, M. H.	"	D	16	"	Sept. 14, 1862	Killed at Crampton's Pass, Md.
380	Vanderburg, Jacob	"	A	33	"	Nov. 16, 1862	Removed from Hagerstown.
484	Voodry, Charles	"	C	94	"	Unknown.	South Mountain.
181	Vetter, Frederick	"	B	149	"	Feb. 23, 1863	Frederick
747	Watson, J. H.			9	"		
765	Walker, Peter	Corporal,	B	103	"	Sept. 17, 1862	Killed in action. Antietam battlefield.
807	Wolf, Henry	"	C	4	"		Antietam battlefield
725	Wagner, Daniel	Private,	G	20	"		"
724	Witt, Louis	"	C	33	"	Sept. 17, 1862	Killed in action. Antietam battlefield.
718	Walby, Howard	"	D	4	"		Antietam battlefield.
715	Wilson, James	"		42	"		"
692	Wands, Charles	"		59	"		"
685	Waler, ——	"		59	"		"
662	Whale, James	"		2	"		"
660	Whaler, John	"		2	"		May be Jas. Whalon. Antietam battlefield.

DESCRIPTIVE LIST.

654	Welden, Charles L.	Private,	F	35	Infantry,	Sept. 17, 1862	Killed in action. Antietam battlefield.
643	Walker, Alex.	"	E	20	"	"	May be Thos. Walker. Antietam battlefield.
632	Whitney, Isaac	"	C	104	"	Sept. 17, 1862	Killed in action. Antietam battlefield.
546	Willis, Ozre	"	H	108	"		
549	Wood, Enory M.	"	C	104	"	Oct. 3, 1862	Died at Pry's Mill, Md. Antietam battlefield.
579	Wasson, Samuel	"	A	89	"	Sept. 17, 1862	Killed in action Antietam.
583	Wood, George	"	F	51	"		
608	Williams, Richard E.	"	E	97	"	Nov. 3, 1862	Smoketown.
610	Wagner, John	"	B	49	"	Feb. 15, 1862	Died U. S. Hospital, Antietam.
611	Wilson, James	"	B	122	"	Nov. 7, 1862	Smoketown.
507	Whitney, John	"	D	103	"	Sept. 17, 1862	Left on battlefield mortally wounded.
491	Whitney, Seldon L.	"	H	22	"	Sept. 14, 1862	Killed at South Mountain.
466	White, Abraham	"	C	143	"		South Mountain.
457	Wools, D. E.	"	E	95	"		Middletown.
419	Wheaton, Frank	"	G	107	"	Oct. 10, 1862	At Harper's Ferry.
317	Wilkins, James	"	K	5	Artillery,		Weverton.
75	Warner, C. M.	"	K	21	Cavalry,	July 16, 1864	Frederick, Md.
351	Willers, John A.	"	K	83	Infantry S. M.		Antietam battlefield.
368	Wright, Rufus C.	"	E	16	"	Nov. 7, 1862	Died at Hagerstown.
370	Ward, David D.	"	K	121	"	Oct. 28, 1862	Died at Bakersville.
393	Wood, Edwin H.	"	D	33	"	Nov. 21, 1862	Hagerstown.
275	Welch, William J.	"	C	88	"	Oct. 18, 1862	Frederick. Rem'd from Frederick, Md.
274	Ward, Morris	"	H	63	"	Oct. 19, 1862	Removed from Frederick.
257	Will, John	"	B	57	"	Oct. 11, 1862	" "
247	Woglen, Samuel	"	G	107	"	Oct. 29, 1862	" "
220	Wayne, Walter G.	"	F	66	"	Nov. 5, 1862	" "
208	Whales, William H.	"	G	4	Artillery,	Dec. 22, 1862	" "
207	Wixon, Daniel B.	"	I	59	"	Dec. 28, 1862	" "
177	Ward, John	"	H	2	"	July 31, 1863	Age 50—Removed from Frederick.
57	Weber, Lewis	"	—	1	Cavalry,	April 5, 1864	Died at Frederick.
58	Weston, J. L.	"	A	1	"	April 15, 1864	Removed from Frederick.
59	Williams, John	"	L	1	"	July 11, 1864	Removed from Frederick.
83	Wordley, Joseph	"	K	151	Infantry,	July 18, 1864	Removed from Frederick.
84	Westcott, Randall H.	"	H	106	"	July 19, 1864	Died at Frederick. Removed from Frederick.
97	Williams, George	"	E	9	Heavy Art'y,	Aug. 4, 1864	Removed from Frederick. [Frederick.
98	Wait, Warran B.	"	K	106	Infantry,	July 30, 1862	Died of wounds at Monocacy. Rem'd from
119	Wilhelm, Jacob	"	C	175,	"	Oct. 12, 1864	Removed from Frederick.
149	Whalen, John	"	G	66	"	Sept. 28, 1862	Removed from Frederick.

84   ANTIETAM NATIONAL CEMETERY.

NEW YORK—Continued.

Headst'e No.	NAME.	Rank.	Company	Regiment.	Arm of Service.	Date of Death.	REMARKS.
167	Whalen, William	Private,	B	68	Infantry,	Oct. 6, 1862	Removed from Frederick.
55	Welch, Daniel	"	F	59	"	Oct. 8, 1862	"
31	Woodworth, Adolphus P.	"	G	193	"	Aug. 16, 1865	Cumberland.
257	Will, John	"	M	49	"	Sept. 17, 1862	Killed in action Antietam.
401	Wood, Nelson	"	C	21	Cavalry,	May 11, 1864	Removed from Downsville.
545	Young, Andrew	"			Infantry,		Antietam battlefield.
196	Young, Harvey	"	B	77	"	Dec. 27, 1862	Frederick.
186	Young, Nicholas	"	A	108	"	Jan. 11, 1863	"
82	Young, David Jr.	Sergeant,	A	106	"	July 22, 1864	Died at Frederick.
395	Zimmerman, Martin B.	Private,	C	9	Infantry,	Aug. 20, 1864	Weverton.
7	Unknown—New York.			9			Removed from Antietam battlefield.
13	Unknown—New York.			61			Removed from Antietam battlefield.
12	Unknown—New York.			88			Removed from Antietam battlefield.
1	Unknown—New York.			108			Removed from Antietam battlefield.
3	Unknown—New York.			2			Removed from Antietam battlefield.
1	Unknown—New York.			28			Removed from Antietam battlefield.
3	Unknown—New York.			121			Removed from Antietam battlefield.
1	Unknown—New York.			89			Removed from Antietam battlefield.
1	Unknown—New York.			107			Removed from Antietam battlefield,
2	Unknown—New York.			16			Removed from Antietam battlefield.
2	Unknown—New York.			6			Removed from Antietam battlefield.
2	Unknown—New York.			5			Removed from Antietam battlefield.
1	Unknown—New York.	Corporal,		9	Battery B		Removed from Antietam battlefield.
2	Unknown—New York.			137	Infantry,		Removed from Antietam battlefield.
1	Unknown—New York.			22	"		Removed from Antietam battlefield.
1	Unknown—New York.			21	"		Removed from Antietam battlefield.
84	Unknown—New York.			51	"		Removed from Antietam battlefield.

DESCRIPTIVE LIST. 85

COMMISSIONED OFFICERS.

"Headst'e" No.	NAME.	Rank.	Company.	Regim't	State.	Date of Death.	REMARKS.
858	Bachelle, Von Werner	Captain,	F	6	Wisconsin,	Sept. 17, 1862	Killed in action Antietam.
859	Bierwith, Francis V.	"	G	69	Pennsylvania,	Sept. 17, 1862	"
866	Brackett, Edward E.	Lieut.	D	10	Maine,	Sept. 17, 1862	"
873	Buffum, George R.	"	D	4	Rhode Island,	Oct. 19, 1862	Removed from Keedysville.
883	Bolza, Charles F.	2d Lieut.			Mich. Cavalry,	July 14, 1863	Killed in action at Falling Waters.
867	Carter, William M.	1st Lieut.	B	8	Pa. Reserves,	Sept. 14, 1862	Removed from Middletown.
882	Collins, John	2d Lieut.		121	New York,		Removed from Weverton.
854	Dexter, Samuel	2d Lieut.	B	42	"	Sept. 17, 1862	Removed from Antietam battlefield.
860	Delorme, Louis	"	H	97	"	Sept. 17, 1862	Removed from Antietam battlefield.
887	Day, Putnam	"		5	Connecticut,	1861	Removed from Frederick.
861	Ellison, ——	Lieut.,		18	Massachusetts,		Removed from Antietam battlefield.
879	Ford, ——	"		17	Michigan,		Rem'd from Keedysville. Cold Water, Mich.
857	Jam, A.	2d Lieut.	E	20	New York,	Sept. 17, 1862	Removed from Antietam battlefield.
875	Kop, Peter	Captain,	B	27	Indiana,	Sept. 17, 1862	Rem'd from Keedysville. From Bloomington.
852	Lantry, John	2d Lieut.	I	8	Ohio,	Sept. 17, 1862	Removed from Antietam battlefield.
870	Loetze, Hugo	1st Lieut.	C	7	New York,	Oct. 24, 1862	Removed from Keedysville.
876	Lee, Jacob A.	1st Lieut.	C	27	Indiana,	Sept. 17, 1862	"
855	McPherson, Charles	Captain,		42	New York,		Removed from Antietam battlefield.
856	Meckback, ——	2d Lieut.,		20	"		Removed from Antietam battlefield.
871	Molkte, Magnus	"		5	Maryland,		Removed from Keedysville.
885	Mott, J. Milton	Captain,	K	5	Wisconsin,	July 26, 1863	Age 45—Died at Frederick.
886	Morris, J. V.	"	M	8	Illinois Cav'y,	July 9, 1864	Removed from Frederick.
881	Priester, Solomon	Lieut.		7	W. Va. Cav'y,		Removed from Berlin.
863	Richerson, J. W.	"		39	Illinois,		Removed from Williamsport.
851	Reed, Alexander N.	1st Lieut.	I	3	Wisconsin,	Sept. 17, 1862	Killed in action at Antietam.
853	Sandford, O. W.	2d Lieut.	I	?		Oct. 13, 1862	Died of wounds received at Antietam.
850	Tarbox, Brainerd D.	Lieut.	B	108	New York,	Sept. 17, 1862	Removed from Boonesboro'.
862	Unknown,	"			Penn. Vols.,		Removed from Antietam battlefield.
864	Unknown,	"					Removed from Antietam battlefield.
868	Unknown,	"					"
869	Unknown,	"		20	New York,		Removed from Keedysville.

86   ANTIETAM NATIONAL CEMETERY.

COMMISSIONED OFFICERS—CONTINUED.

Headst'e No.	NAME	Rank	Company	Reg'me't	State	Date of Death	REMARKS
877	Unknown,	Lieut.		17	Michigan,		Removed from Keedysville.
878	Unknown,	"		17	"		"
880	Unknown;	"					
865	Wade, William	2d Lieut.	I	10	Maine,	Sept. 17, 1862	Removed from Antietam battlefield.
872	Wilson, William	"	B	71	Pennsylvania,	Sept. 21, 1862	Removed from Keedysville.
874	Wimpfheimer, Max	Lieut.	G	2	Pa. Reserves,	Sept. 17, 1862	"
884	Williams, S.	"			Cavalry.		Removed from Cavetown.

OHIO.

Headst'e No.	NAME	Rank	Company	Reg'me't	Arm of Service.	Date of Death	REMARKS
1172	Auker, Edwin R.	Private,	G	193	Infantry,	Mar. 27, 1865	Clarysville.
1171	Arnold, Charles F.	"	C	96	"	Apr. 17, 1865	"
1163	Ackley, Wesley	"	E	36	"	Aug. 5, 1864	"
1241	Adamson, Robert	"	I	67	"		Cumberland.
1326	Armstrong, Joshua A.	Sergeant,	F	23	"	Sept. 17, 1862	Removed from Antietam battlefield.
1345	Armstrong, John W.	Private,	E	5	"	Sept. 17, 1862	Removed from Antietam battlefield.
1379	Allton, J. E.	"	D	30	"		Removed from South Mountain.
1428	Anderson, John	"	K	36	"	Sept. 14, 1862	"
1453	Anderson, John S.	"	A	123	"	Aug. 10, 1862	Removed from Middletown.
1510	Austin, J. A.	"	F	29	"	April 2, 1862	Removed from Weverton.
1174	Bingman, Ezra	"	G	151	N. Guards,	July 5, 1864	Clarysville.
1169	Battie, David	"	D	55	Infantry,	July 21, 1862	"
1167	Borg, Peter	Sergeant,	D	165	N. Guards,	Aug. 18, 1864	"
1160	Bland, David	Private,	G	191	Infantry,	Apr. 14, 1865	"
1155	Brooks, Virgil	"	A	92	"	April 18, 1865	"

DESCRIPTIVE LIST.

1199	Brainard, Oliver	Private,	F	161 N. Guards,		May 28,	1864 Cumberland.
1206	Bellman, Lewis	"	E	55 Infantry,		July 11,	1862 "
1209	Bosley, Thomas	"	B	34 "			"
1211	Burk, Joseph	"	G	69 "			"
1219	Ballard, Franklin	"	F	67 "			"
1229	Burd, Samuel	"	G	67 "			"
1233	Bennett, Charles W.	"	D	116 "		Dec. 12,	1862 "
1245	Baker, Stephen	"	F	116 "		April 12,	1863 "
1247	Behme, Frederick	"	K	67 "			"
1248	Bruce, Abram	"	H	91 "		Aug. 14,	1864 "
1322	Beath, Granville	"	L	149 N. Guards,		Aug. 21,	1864 Frederick.
1294	Badger, Oliver	"	A	126 Infantry,		July 20,	1864 "
1271	Biegler, John	"	K	192 "		Mar. 27,	1864 .
1340	Briggs, John	Sergeant,	D	8 "		Sept. 17,	1862 Removed from Antietam battlefield.
1350	Bacon, Henry	Private,	H	7 "		Sept. 17,	1862 Removed from Antietam battl-field.
1357	Boughton, Charles W.	Corporal,	H	8 "		Sept. 21,	1862 Removed from Antietam battlefield.
1376	Ball, John	Private,	L	1 Artillery,		Sept. 26,	1862 Removed from Smoketown.
1420	Baker, John	"	E	11 Infantry,		Sept. 14,	1862 Removed from South Mountain.
1417	Boss, John	"	K	11 "		Sept. 18,	1862 "
1416	Brooks, Jonas	"	B	12 "		Sept. 14,	1862 "
1405	Bollinger, Jacob	"	K	45 "			
1404	Brookman, Charles V.	"	C	23 "		Sept. 22,	1862 Removed from Middletown.
1402	Barnes, Joshua L.	"	A	23 "		Sept. 14,	1862 "
1394	Beth, Peter	"	H	160 "		Aug. 15,	1864 "
1391	Boyd, J. W.	"	H	135 N. Guards,			
1387	Boshler, Thomas						
1460	Buskirk, William S.	"	E	116 Infantry,		Aug. 26,	1864 Removed from Weverton.
1477	Bryant, Jesse	"	K	8 Cavalry,		Sept. 12,	1864 Removed from Hagerstown.
1479	Bullfinch, Byron	"	K	29 Infantry,		Oct. 28,	1862 Removed from Frederick.
1488	Brownell, Jasper	"	F	4 "		Dec. 24,	1862 Removed from Frederick.
1493	Buckley, John	"	C	87 "		Sept. 25,	1862 Removed from Frederick.
1502	Britch, George	"	C	55 "		July 14,	1862 Removed from Frederick.
1500	Bossler, Jonas	"	F	8 "		Sept. 6,	1862 Removed from Frederick.
1170	Cline, David	"	H	19 "		June 23,	1865 Removed from Clarysville.
1161	Cotton, Elisha			36 "		Mar. 3,	1865 "
1158	Cook, William	"	K	156 N. Guards,		Aug. 10,	1864 "
1157	Carpenter, Octavius	"	F	193 Infantry,		May 10,	1865 "
1200	Clute, John	"	E	36 "		Dec. 31,	1864 Removed from Cumberland.

OHIO—CONTINUED.

Headst'e No.	NAME.	Rank.	Company	Regiment	Arm of Service.	Date of Death.	REMARKS.
1207	Cooper, Francis	Private,	B	122	Infantry,	Jan. 28, 1863	Removed from Cumberland.
1214	Comstock, Josephus	"	G	116	"	Dec. 16, 1862	"
1230	Cameron, Joseph L.	Corporal,	I	67	"		"
1234	Carter, James	Private,	B	67	"		"
1255	Carney, John A.	"	G	96	"		"
1318	Crossan, Alexander	"	E	34	"	Aug. 24, 1864	Removed from Frederick.
1311	Clegg, Moses	Corporal,	E	16	"	Oct. 13, 1864	"
1298	Craig, Franklin	Private,	K	149	N. Guards,	July 9, 1864	"
1291	Coburn, William T.	"	H	126	Infantry,	July 16, 1864	"
1274	Carter, James	"	B	192	"	April 19, 1865	"
1270	Chivens, Hiram W.	"	A	194	"	Mar. 30, 1865	"
1264	Cronch, George	"	H	75	"	July 28, 1862	"
1332	Cole, Orville B.	"	G	7	"	Sept. 17, 1862	Removed from Antietam battlefield.
1349	Carter, James B.	Sergeant,	F	8	"	Sept. 17, 1862	Removed from Antietam battlefield.
1356	Conner, John M.	Private,		7	"	Sept. 21, 1862	Removed from Antietam battlefield.
1373	Coe, Alson	"	G	12	"	Sept. 14, 1862	Removed from Smoketown.
1415	Cockrille, William	"	C	170	N. Guards,	Aug. 14, 1864	Removed from South Mountain.
1468	Carpenter, George	"	C	36	Infantry,	Sept. 14, 1862	Removed from Weverton.
1496	Cherrington, Spencer	"	K	196	"	May 24, 1865	Removed from Frederick.
1154	Ducia, Anthony	"	C	196	"	April 22, 1865	Removed from Clarysville.
1152	Dewey, Daniel D.	"	E	29	"	Mar. 8, 1862	"
1217	Davis, Euthen	"	F	9	"	Feb. 28, 1862	Removed from Cumberland.
1222	Davidson, James S.	"	F	29	"		Removed from Cumberland.
1235	Dimock, Franklin	"	F	29	"	Apr. 1, 1862	Removed from Cumberland.
1251	Dudley, Charles E.	"	I	91	"	Nov. 1, 1864	Removed from Cumberland.
1309	Downey, Henry	"	K	170	N. Guards,	July 28, 1864	Removed from Frederick.
1300	Dunlap, William	"	B	194	Infantry,	Mar. 30, 1865	Removed from Frederick.
1273	Dye, James	"	I		"		Removed from Frederick.
1437	Dunn, John	"		23	"		Removed from South Mountain.
1434	Dixon, Robert A.	"		23	"	Sept. 15, 1862	Removed from South Mountain.
1431	Daley, Andrew J.	"	K	36	"	Sept. 14, 1862	Removed from South Mountain.

DESCRIPTIVE LIST.

	Name	Rank	Co.	Regt.	Date	Remarks
1421	Debretz, Michael	Corporal,	K	11 Infantry,	Sept. 14, 1862	Removed from South Mountain
1411	D——, J. H.	Private,		11 "	"	"
1409	Detrick, George	"	D	5 "	Aug. 10, 1864	Removed from Middletown.
1388	Davis, George H.	"	B	23 "	Oct. 12, 1864	Removed from Weverton.
1454	Davis, Miles H.	"	C	116 "	Sept. 25, 1864	"
1465	Dierkes, Charles	"	E	116 "	Sept. 22, 1864	"
1466	Dunn, Calvin	"	D	123 "	Sept. 15, 1864	"
1469	Donevan, William	"	K	126 "	Mar. 13, 1865	Removed from Clarysville.
1162	Erskine, Lewis	"	D	23 "	July 28, 1864	"
1150	Eoff, Leander	"	E	116 "	Aug. 9, 1864	"
1258	Eno, Cleophas	"	B	91 "		
1342	Eyton, Henry	"		5 "	Oct. 5, 1862	Removed from Antietam battlefield.
1360	Eldridge, James V.	"	D	23 "	Sept. 21, 1862	Removed from Antietam battlefield.
1364	Ewers, Edmund Jr.	"	D	30 "	Oct. 6, 1862	Removed from Antietam battlefield.
1375	Everitt, David	"	E	7 "	Sept. 14, 1862	Removed from Smoketown.
1430	Edmunson, Theodore	"	C	36 "		"
1401	Edwards, William	"	F	23 "		Removed from Middletown.
1395	Edgerly, Amos	"	D	135 N. Guards,	July 7, 1864	"
1168	Furst, John	"	C	191 Infantry,	April 19, 1865	Removed from Clarysville.
1166	Fremas, William	"		7 "		Removed from Cumberland.
1213	Fowler, Mead	"	I	67 "		
1260	Fitzpatrick, John	"	F	8 N. Guards,	Sept. 17, 1862	Removed from Clarysville.
1334	Fields, John S.	"	L	161 N. Guards,	Aug. 8, 1864	Removed from Antietam battlefield.
1316	Flenner, L. G.	"	I	5 Infantry,	Oct. 1, 1862	Removed from Frederick.
1341	Fitzgibbons, Patrick	Corporal,	E	11 "	Sept. 17, 1862	Removed from Antietam battlefield.
1366	Ferry, Amos	Private,	I	112 N. Guards,	Aug. 12, 1864	Removed from Antietam battlefield.
1450	Fleak, William	"	B	122 Infantry,	July 15, 1863	Removed from Middletown.
1471	Ferguson, James	"		"		Removed from Weverton.
1156	G——, P.	"		"		Removed from Oakland.
1205	Gray, John M.	"	L	184 "	July 6, 1864	Removed from Cumberland.
1286	Goodbrane, Alfred	"	D	161 N. Guards,	Sept. 17, 1862	Removed from Frederick.
1324	Goodman, Mabery	"	E	23 Infantry,	Sept. 17, 1862	Removed from Antietam b. g.
1327	Goodloe, Viran	Corporal,	C	12 "	Sept. 17, 1862	"
1348	Gutzler, Jacob	Private,	A	5 "	Sept. 17, 1862	"
1374	Goodsell, Edward W.	Corporal,	C	7 "	Sept. 14, 1862	Removed from Smoketown.
1432	Gibbons, Henry J.	Private,	G	36 "	Aug. 19, 1862	Removed from South Mountain.
1397	Garrett, Andrew	"	E	160 N. Guards,	Aug. 19, 1864	Removed from Middletown.
1480	Gentle, George W.	"	E	5 Infantry,	Sept. 17, 1862	Removed from Frederick.

ANTIETAM NATIONAL CEMETERY.

OHIO—Continued.

Headst'e No.	NAME.	Rank.	Company	Regime't	Arm of Service.	Date of Death.	REMARKS.
1489	Gray, William E.	Sergeant,	K	29	Infantry,	Dec. 10, 1862	Removed from Frederick.
1220	Halpin, William P.	Private,	G	192	"	April 25, 1865	Removed from Clarysville.
1317	Hill, Ely J.	"	A	116	"	Aug. 31, 1864	Removed from Frederick.
1315	Hoesch, George	"	E	110	"	Aug. 8, 1864	"
1292	Harley, W.	"	B	149	N. Guards,	July 23, 1864	"
1290	Howell, James	Sergeant,	E	110	Infantry,	July 11, 1864	"
1328	Hamman, John	Private,	A	11	"		
1343	Harbin, John W.	"	C	116	"	Aug. 6, 1863	Removed from Antietam battlefield.
1369	Howard, George	"	B	5	"	Sept. 19, 1862	Removed from Antietam battlefield.
1400	Harper, Wilson B.	"	H	23	"		Removed from Smoketown.
1452	Holnman, Peter	"	H	123	"		Removed from Middletown.
1456	Hatfield, ——	"	D		"	Sept. 10, 1864	"
1464	Hailton, William	"	D	23	"	Apr. 7, 1864	Removed from Weverton.
1494	Hess, William	"	F	30	"	Nov. 13, 1864	"
1497	Hoover, John W.	"	K	36	"	Sept. 30, 1864	Removed from Frederick.
1513	Hull, Samuel H.	"	H	116	"	Sept. 14, 1862	"
1175	Irwin, David	"	K	36	"	Aug. 4, 1864	Removed from Weverton.
1212	Ives, William C.	"	A	29	"	July 24, 1864	Removed from Clarysville.
1511	Inman, J. R.	"			Teamster,	Mar. 5, 1862	Removed from Cumberland.
1224	Johnson, Ira	"	B	67	Infantry,	Mar. 23, 1862	Removed from Frederick.
1252	Johnson, William	"	E	29	"		Removed from Cumberland.
1307	Johnson, Abram S.	"	A	23	"	April 10, 1862	Removed from Frederick.
1266	Jones, John	"	I	191	"	Oct. 17, 1864	"
1412	Jadwin, Isaac	"	D	30	"	April 4, 1865	"
1397	Jobenour, J.	"		5	"	Sept. 14, 1862	Removed from South Mountain. F'm Hardin Co.
1462	Johnson, Thomas	"	K	170	"	Aug. 11, 1864	Removed from Middletown.
1227	Koons, John	"	G	110	"	Mar. 1, 1863	Removed from Weverton.
1244	Kanas, James P.	"		7	"		Removed from Cumberland.
1283	Kregen, Frank	"	H	110	"	July 9, 1864	Removed from Frederick.
1280	Kemp, Charles	"	E	192	"	Apr. 19, 1865	"
1267	Knapp, Brundage	"	I	55	"	Aug. 12, 1862	"

DESCRIPTIVE LIST.

#	Name	Rank	Co.	Regt.	Date	Year	Remarks
1333	Keeran, John	Private,	G	8 Infantry,	Sept. 17,	1862	Removed from Antietam battlefield.
1352	Kendall, Lorenzo	"	K	"	Sept. 17,	1862	Removed from Antietam battlefield.
1372	Kohler, John J.	"	L	"	Oct. 14,	1862	Removed from Smoketown.
1447	Kinniston, W. W.	"	K	"	Sept. 14,	1862	Removed from South Mountain.
1393	Kelly, Isaac	"	H	160 N. Guards,	Aug. 17,	1864	Removed from Middletown.
1472	Kennedy, Ira	"	F	1 Light Battery,	Oct. 6,	1862	Removed from Hagerstown.
1164	Light, Mathias	"	D	116 Infantry,	July 8,	1864	Removed from Clarysville.
1232	Laken, John	"	B	"	Feb. 13,	1862	Removed from Cumberland.
1149	Lyons, William	"	I	34	Aug. 26,	1864	Removed from Clarysville.
1218	Lockmiller, James	"					Removed from Cumberland.
1238	Lentz, John H.	"	K	126	Feb. 18,	1863	"
1242	Loomis, Joseph	"	G	29	Feb. 26,	1862	"
1243	Lyon, Lewis	"					
1257	Liebe, Joseph	"	D	123	July 16,	1864	Removed from Clarysville.
1223	Love, James	"	H	126	Sept. 3,	1864	Removed from Frederick.
1313	Long, Daniel	"	F	23	Aug. 26,	1864	"
1308	Larrick, Benjamin	"	H	116	Oct. 2,	1864	"
1304	Lynch, J. W.	"	E	23	Sept. 26,	1864	"
1301	Labrie, Octave	"			July 23,	1864	"
1282	Large, Benjamin F.	"	H	126	July 21,	1863	Age 18—Removed from Frederick.
1272	Lewis, William C.	Corporal,	D	194	Apr. 9,	1865	Removed from Frederick.
1268	Lapham, Amza	Private,	K		Aug. 6,	1862	"
1266	Lambright, Isaac	"	G	55	Sept. 3,	1862	"
1344	Long, Charles M.	Corporal,	F		Sept. 17,	1862	Removed from Antietam battlefield.
1406	Lindley, John H.	Sergeant,	E	23			Removed from South Mountain.
1399	Light, Henry C.	Private,	D	23			Removed from Middletown.
1458	Leeper, Arch'd	"	I	12			Removed from Weverton.
1461	Lanning, George	Sergeant,	K	170 N. Guards,			
1482	Lucas, Elisha	Private,	H	4 Infantry,	Sept. 1,	1864	Removed from Frederick.
1470	Lambert, Joseph	Corporal,	B	91	Dec. 4,	1862	Removed from Weverton.
1151	Morgan, David B.	Private,	F	193	Sept. 16,	1864	Removed from Clarysville.
1148	Moore, John	"	A	92	May 23,	1865	"
1198	McKay, William	"	H	67	May 15,	1865	
1203	McFarland, Archibald	Sergeant,	B	110			Removed from Cumberland.
1210	Mowser, Irvin	Private,	H	66	Jan. 18,	1863	"
1225	McGee, John	"	G	110	Feb. 23,	1862	"
1228	Marsh, Thadeus	"	H	29	Dec. 10,	1862	"
1239	Metzker, Samuel	"	G	8	Mar. 1,	1862	

OHIO—CONTINUED.

Head'st'e No.	NAME.	Rank.	Company	Reg'ment	Arm of Service.	Date of Death.	REMARKS.
1246	Mathes, Albert	Private,	A	174	Infantry,	Feb. 27, 1865	Removed from Clarysville.
1263	Miller, John R.	Corporal,	D	87	"	Sept. 19, 1862	Removed from Frederick.
1351	Meacham, Eldridge F.	Private,	B	7	"	Sept. 17, 1862	Removed from Antietam battlefield.
1354	Miller, John	"	F	5	"	Sept. 17, 1862	Removed from Antietam battlefield.
1368	Morris, William Edward	"	—	66	"	Sept. 17, 1862	Removed from Smoketown.
1371	Mouser, Casper	"	G	66	"	Oct. 10, 1862	Removed from Smoketown.
1439	McKirtrick, William	"	K	30	"	Sept. 14, 1862	Removed from South Mountain.
1414	McCreara, James	"	C	11	"	Sept. 14, 1862	"
1455	McKenzie, James T.	1st Serg't,	G	116	"	Aug. 24, 1864	Removed from Weverton.
	Mercer, William H. H.	Private,	F	170	N. Guards,		"
1473	McCune, Edward B.	"	B	36	Infantry,	Oct. 13, 1862	Removed from Antietam battlefield.
1481	McFadden, John	Sergeant,	L	7	"	Oct. 30, 1862	Removed from Frederick.
1483	Mann, William R.	Private,	H	8	"	Nov. 30, 1862	Removed from Frederick.
1490	McNaughton, Abram W.	"	A	29	"	Jan. 28, 1862	Removed from Frederick.
1504	Montgomery, H.	"			"	Jan. 4, 1862	Removed from Frederick.
1506	McFall, Robert	"	B	29	"	June 27, 1862	Removed from Frederick.
1507	Monett, G. T. B.	"	E	66	"	April 15, 1862	Removed from Frederick.
1153	Newell, Thomas J.	Sergean,	K	194	"	April 23, 1865	Removed from Clarysville.
1314	Neal, John B.	Private,	B	91	"	Sept. 21, 1864	Removed from Frederick.
1261	Noble, John	"	F	11	"	Sept. 2, 1862	"
1355	Nichols, Frederick E.	"	C	8	"	Sept. 17, 1862	Removed from Antietam battlefield.
1403	Noble, William	"	D	30	"	Oct. 11, 1862	Removed from Middletown.
1499	Nobles, John	"	D	50	"	Sept. 14, 1862	Removed from Frederick.
1495	Newell, D. D.						
1201	Oty, Henry	"	C	194	"	April 14, 1865	Removed from Clarysville.
1312	Oliver, Henry	"	F	36	"	Sept. 1, 1864	Removed from Frederick.
1408	O'Hara, ——	"	G	29	"		Removed from South Mountain.
1503	O'Conner, N.				"		Removed from Frederick.
1143	Pennock, Jacob	"	F	196	"	July 3, 1862	Removed from Frederick.
1204	Percefield, John	"	H	91	"	April 26, 1864	Removed from Clarysville.
1240	Price, John	"	B	62	"	July 24, 1864	Removed from Cumberland.
						Feb. 26, 1862	

DESCRIPTIVE LIST.

No.	Name	Rank	Co.	Regt.	Date	Remarks
1250	Pearson, William	Sergeant,	I	152 N. Guards,	Aug. 2, 1864	Removed from Cumberland.
1306	Pero, William	Private,	G	122 Infantry,	Nov. 14, 1864	Removed from Frederick.
1296	Peyton, Andrew J.	"	B	126 "	July 18, 1864	"
1285	Parker, Isaac N.	"	H	126 "	July 18, 1864	"
1336	Palmerton, William S.	"	F	8 "	Sept. 17, 1862	Removed from Antietam battlefield. Age 16 – Rem'd f'm Middletown. F'm Eaton.
1398	Phillips, Edgar A.	"	K	161 "	April 16, 1864	Removed from Weverton.
1467	Pole, Gabriel	"	D	123 "	Oct. 20, 1862	Removed from Frederick.
1478	Pierce, Sylvester	"	K	29 "	Sept. 14, 1862	"
1498	Parsons, Henry W.	"	H	23 "	July 16, 1864	"
1297	Rooks, G. B.	"	E	122 "		"
1358	Reynolds, J. K.	Sergeant,				
1236	Ritter, William L.	Private,	K	126 "	Nov. 26, 1862	Removed from Cumberland.
1254	Ross, John	"	F	91 "	Aug. 16, 1861	"
1259	Recer, Jacob	"	E	34 "	Oct. 19, 1864	Removed from Clarysville.
1303	Rickabaugh, John H.	"	K	91 "	Nov. 7, 1864	Removed from Frederick.
1277	Rainey, John W.	"	C	195 "	April 13, 1865	Removed from Cumberland.
1339	Richardson, William P.	"	A	8 "	Sept. 17, 1862	Removed from Antietam battlefield.
1262	Ring, Jonathan	"		8 "		Removed from Antietam battlefield.
1362	Reichmann, Jacob	"	H	12 "	Sept. 19, 1862	Removed from Antietam battlefield.
1448	Rice, William	"	K	36 "	Sept. 15, 1862	Removed from South Mountain.
1407	Richardson, Daniel J.	"	H	23 "	Sept. 27, 1862	"
1491	Riggle, Thomas	"	G	122 "	Aug. 14, 1863	Age 21 – Removed from Frederick.
1509	Rosel, William	"	K	7 "	June 1, 1862	Removed from Frederick.
1145	Surenkamp, Henry	"	C	28 "	Feb. 2, 1865	Removed from Clarysville.
1144	Smith, Simpson	"	L	1 Artillery,	April 14, 1864	"
1215	Stoll, Frederick	"	L	3 Cavalry,		Removed from Cumberland.
1221	Stewart, Charles	"	H	122 Infantry,	Jan. 24, 1863	"
1223	Shannon, James	"	A	123 "	Dec. 29, 1862	"
1231	Stoneking, James A.	"	H	116 "	Nov. 30, 1862	"
1237	Spitter, Isaiah	"	K	91 "		"
1253	Stewart, Frank M.	"	K	67 "	Mar. 6, 1862	"
1321	Scarburg, Zachariah	"	E	2 Cavalry,	Sept. 7, 1864	Removed from Frederick.
1320	Sieers, Isaac M.	"	A	160 N. Guards,	July 31, 1864	"
1299	Schweitzer, Samuel, Jr.	"	B	161 "	July 29, 1864	"
1289	Sawhill, Alexander J.	"	D	122 Infantry,	July 15, 1864	"
1288	Slater, O.	"	I	106 "	July 12, 1864	"
1278	Steel, John H.	"		194 "	Apr. 19, 1865	"
1265	Smith, B. F.	"	F	23 "	Sept. 22, 1862	"

94   ANTIETAM NATIONAL CEMETERY.

OHIO—CONTINUED.

Headst'e No.	NAME.	Rank.	Company	Reg'ment	Arm of Service.	Date of Death.	REMARKS.
1330	Spain, David R.	Corporal,	F	23	Infantry,	Sept. 17, 1862	Removed from Antietam battlefield.
1347	Spellman, William	Private,	E	5	"	Sept. 17, 1862	Removed from Antietam battlefield.
1353	Sherrick, George O.	"	B	7	"	Sept. 17, 1862	Removed from Antietam battlefield.
1363	Sherrow, Laban	"	—	12	"		Removed from Antietam battlefield.
1367	Scherlott, John	"	G	30	"	Oct. 20, 1862	Removed from Antietam battlefield.
1446	Shed, S.	"		36	"		Removed from South Mountain.
1445	Simmons, L. B.	"	K	36	"	Sept. 14, 1862	"
1433	Sim, Edmund A.	"	D	23	"	Sept. 14, 1852	"
1424	S——, T.	"		20	"		"
1415	Schlosser, John	"	K	11	"	Sept. 17, 1862	"
1484	Scott, Mark	"	D	4	"	Nov. 27, 1862	Removed from Frederick.
1501	Swearinger, George W.	"	A	60	"	July 10, 1862	"
1508	Salisbury, Norman	"	H	29	"	April 3, 1862	"
1165	Tennis, James	"	G	156	N. Guards,	Aug. 18, 1864	Removed from Cumberland.
1159	Taylor, John	"	I	91	Infantry,	Aug. 10, 1864	Removed from Clarysville.
1202	Taylor, Watson	"	F	153	N. Guards,		Removed from Cumberland.
1208	Turner, J. W.	"	D	126	Infantry,		"
1310	Thornton, James	"	B	126	"	Oct. 28, 1854	Removed from Frederick.
1284	Trail, Noah	"	H	126	"	Jan. 15, 1864	"
1281	Thorn, Isaac W.	"	D	194	"	Apr. 1, 1865	"
1275	Tilley, James E.	"	K	194	"	Mar. 31, 1865	"
1337	Trube, Franklin	Corporal,	E	8	"	Sept. 17, 1862	Removed from Antietam batt'efield.
1346	Thompson, William H.	"	H	122	"	Aug. 5, 1862	Removed from Antietam battlefield.
1361	Taylor, David	"	I	30	"	Sept. 17, 1862	Removed from Antietam battlefield.
1419	Tapley, George S.	Private,	B	11	"	Sept. 14, 1862	Removed from South Mountain.
1389	Trochler, George	"	H	149	"	Aug. 6, 1864	Removed from Middletown.
1276	Vandergrif, Samuel	"	H	29	"	April 19, 1865	Removed from Frederick.
1505	Vanscoit, William H.	"	B	116	"	April 5, 1862	Removed from Frederick.
1173	Winland, John H.	"	D	161	N. Guards,	Dec. 6, 1864	Removed from Frederick.
1147	Williams, Elijah	Corporal,	A	161	N. Guards,	July 5, 1864	Removed from Clarysville.
1146	Warren, George G.	Private,	G	123	Infantry,	Jan. 4, 1864	"

DESCRIPTIVE LIST.   95

No.	Name	Rank	Co.	Regiment	Date	Remarks
1216	Walker, Moses	Private,	B	110 Infantry,	Dec. 31, 1862	Removed from Cumberland.
1226	Williams, George A. F.	"	C	1 Cavalry,	"	"
1249	Waters, H. S.	"	F	196 Infantry,	"	"
1422	Wright, G. W.	"	H	11 "	Unknown,	Removed from South Mountain.
1256	Wikle, Martin	"	E	69 "	Sept. 10, 1864	Removed from Cumberland.
1319	Ward, John	"	E	91 "	Dec. 18, 1864	Removed from Frederick.
1305	Welsh, Patrick	"	B	110 "	July 9, 1864	"
1302	Wall, Clarence	"	B	149 N. Guards,	July 19, 1864	"
1295	Walters, Jonathan	"	I	144 "	Aug. 16, 1864	"
1293	White, Madison I.	"	F	91 Infantry,	July 7, 1864	"
1287	White, Isaac M.	Corporal,	I	160 N. Guards,	April 19, 1865	"
1279	Windom, Uriah B.	Private,	I	36 Infantry,	Sept. 17, 1862	Removed from Antietam battlefield.
1325	Wagner, Joseph	"	K	23 "	Sept. 17, 1862	"
1329	Werner, John	"	K	11 "	Nov. 22, 1862	"
1331	Wiswall, James H.	Sergeant,	H	8 "	Sept. 17, 1862	"
1335	West, Albert D.	"	H	8 "	Sept. 21, 1862	"
1359	Wolfe, Henry F.	Private,	A	30 "	Sept. 17, 1862	"
1365	Went, Lewis	"			Nov. 27, 1862	Removed from Smoketown.
1370	Westerman, George	Corporal,			Sept. 14, 1862	Removed from South Mountain.
1458	Whitney, Isaac N.	Private,			Sept. 14, 1862	Removed from South Mountain.
1435	Whisler, Daniel	"			Aug. 24, 1864	Removed from Middletown.
1451	Warner, Daniel	"				Removed from Weverton.
1463	Windsor, Frank M.	"			Nov. 26, 1862	Removed from Frederick.
1485	Walduck, John	"			Dec. 12, 1862	Removed from Frederick.
1486	Wise, Demas C.	"			Nov. 16, 1862	Removed from Frederick. [1862.
1487	Welchance, Lafayette	"			July 18, 1863	Age 21—Rem'd f'm Fred'k. When enlisted,
1492	Williams, Isaac	"			Sept. 17, 1862	Removed from Antietam battlefield.
1338	Yongker, David	"				Removed from Weverton.
1459	Youngblud, Jacob	"			Sept. 4, 1864	Removed from South Mountain, Middletown, Hagerstown and Weverton, Md.
29	Unknown—Ohio.					

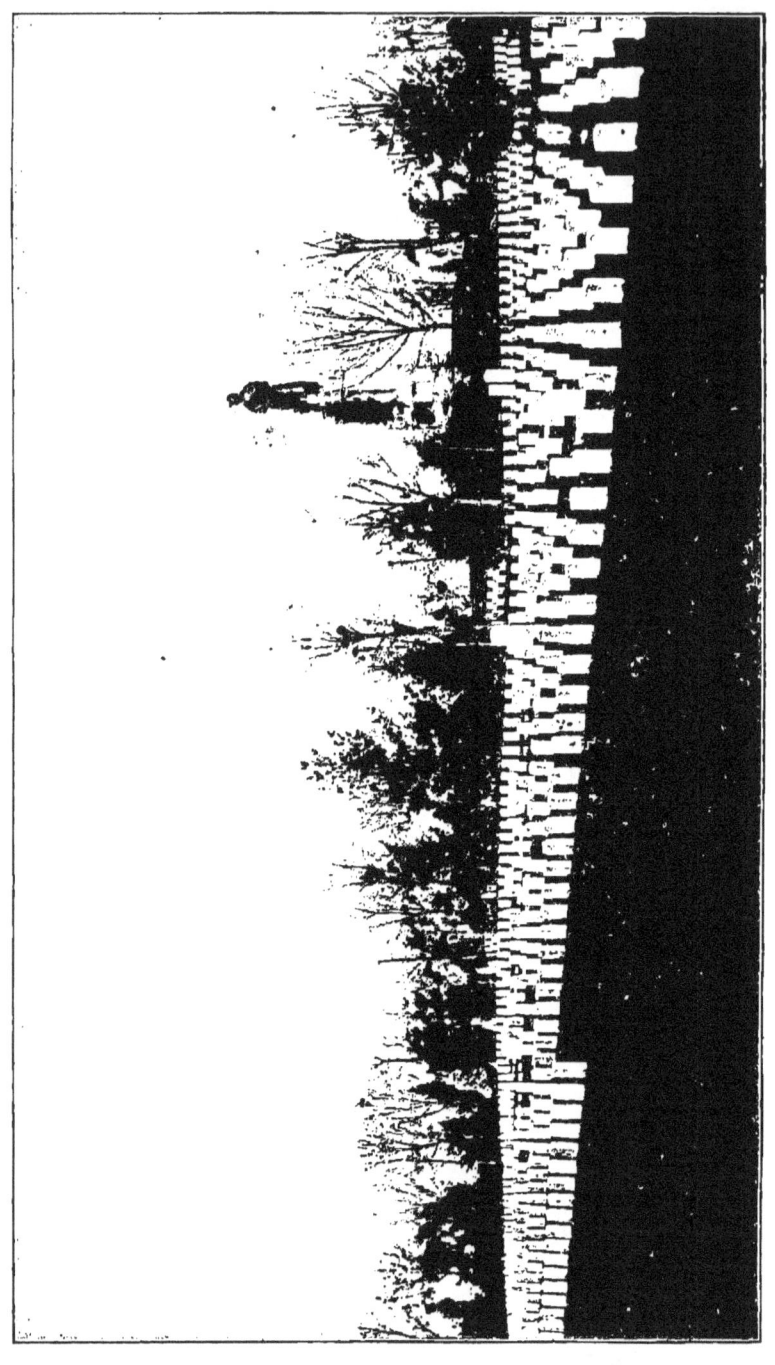

PENNSYLVANIA SECTION.

PENNSYLVANIA.

Head'st No.	NAME	Rank	Company	Regiment	Arm of Service	Date of Death	REMARKS
3779	Allison, James	Private,	A	12	Inf. Reserves,	Unknown,	Antietam battlefield.
3601	Adams, Joseph	Sergeant,	L	155	Infantry,	Oct. 26, 1862	"
3602	Anderson, S. P.	Private,	D	118	"	Sept. 22, 1862	"
3661	Alderman, L. F.	"	I	111	"		
3664	Abbott, L. A.	Corporal,		111	"		
3753	Armor, John R.	Private,	K	111	"	Sept. 18, 1862	"
3716	Anderson, John	"	D	111	"	Oct. 14, 1862	Smoketown.
3812	Anthony, John	"	H	111	"	Oct. 22, 1862	"
4033	Austin, Castil	"	B	7	Inf. Reserves,		Middletown.
4040	Aderhold, Frederick	"	C	7	Inf. Reserves,	Nov. 18, 1862	Age 27. Frederick
4112	Albaugh, Levi	"	L	54	Infantry,	Sept. 24, 1864	Frederick.
4124	Aker, William	"	H	87	"	Jan. 5, 1865	"
4196	Adler, Ambrose J.	"			"	Mar. 4, 1862	Knapp's Battery. Frederick.
3585	Benson, Aaron	"	K	45	"		Antietam battlefield.
3598	Brown, Adam	"		130	"	Sept. 17, 1862	"
3612	Bailey, John	"		8	Cav. or Resv's,		"
3617	Broadbent, John	"		48	Infantry,		"
3620	Beck, Isaac	"		51	"		"
3636	Blackhead, Adam	"		28	"		"
3653	Brown, D. I.	Corporal,	D	111	"	Sept. 17, 1862	"
3663	Buskirk, J. Van	Private,	C	111	"	Sept. 17, 1862	"
3665	Brown, J. A.	"			"		"
3673	Burdick, Albert	"	G	111	"	Feb. 11, 1863	"
3801	Baker, Marion M.	"	G	155	"	Oct. 3, 1862	"
3796	Barr, Daniel	"			"		"
3789	Barns, James A.	"	C	12	Inf. Reserves,	Sept. 17, 1862	"
3778	Bingham, James	"	G	3	"	Sept. 17, 1862	"
3757	Beatty, Henry	"		9	"	Sept. 17, 1862	"
3740	Blanchard, Oliver	"	C	132	Infantry,	Sept. 24, 1862	"
3737	Bryan, J. I.	Corporal,		4	Cav. Reserves,		"
3733	Baker, John	Private,		1	Inf. Reserves,		"

ANTIETAM NATIONAL CEMETERY.

PENNSYLVANIA—CONTINUED.

Head'st No.	NAME	Rank	Company	Reg'ht	Arm of Service	Date of Death			REMARKS
3732	Barr, Jacob W.	Private,	G	137	Infantry,	Oct.	9,	1862	Antietam battlefield.
3718	Bub, George	"	A	12	Cavalry,	Dec.	21,	1862	Smoketown.
3704	Bowen, A. C.	"		124	Infantry,				"
3709	Benson, Enoch	"	H	12	Inf. Reserves,	Nov.	12,	1862	"
3705	Bogart, C. H.	"	F	4	"	Nov.	5,	1862	"
3808	Barnes, Samuel	"	F	9	"	Nov.	2,	1862	"
3815	Beyers, John	"	C						
3820	Bonham, Charlton L.	Corporal,	K	6	Cavalry,	July	11,	1863	Antietam battlefield.
3847	Barnett, John	Private,		9	Inf. Reserves,				South Mountain.
3865	Balleony, John	"	C	45	Infantry,				"
3873	Baird, James	"	H	45	"				"
3895	Burr, Aaron	"		8	Inf. Reserves,				"
3900	Brooks, George W.	"		100	Infantry,				Middletown.
3919	Brown, J. R.	"	C	1	Artillery,	Aug.	20,	1863	Burkettsville.
4018	Brown, Edward	"	C	13	Cavalry,	Aug.	2,	1864	Weverton.
4012	Baker, Albert	"	C	22	"	Mar.		1864	"
3997	Bane, S. J.	"		50					Antietam battlefield.
3979	Bennett, James	"	F	137	Infantry,	Nov.	11,	1862	Hagerstown.
3970	Brown, Ralsten	"	D	139	"	Nov.	11,	1862	Age 23—Hagerstown.
3960	Boreland, James T.	"	L	139	"	Oct.	16,	1862	Age 22—Hagerstown.
3948	Beebe, Oliver	"	D	7	Inf. Reserves,				Antietam battlefield.
3945	Bryson, John	"	D	81	Infantry,	Oct.	15,	1862	Frederick.
3937	Black, Mathew	"	G	45	"	Oct.	14,	1862	"
3936	Bartlett, George L.	"	D	3	"	Oct.	20,	1862	"
3932	Bidwell, Hiram	"	K	48	"	Nov.	14,	1862	"
4041	Burke, Peter	"	F	111	"	Jan.	22,	1863	"
4064	Booles, Amos	"	G	111	"	Feb.	8,	1863	"
4068	Burdick, Albert	"	D	2	Artillery	April	17,	1866	Removed from Hagerstown.
4226	Blair, Edwin B.	"	A	136	Infantry,	Feb.	1,	1863	Frederick.
4066	Burgess, John	"	A	14	Cavalry,	Aug.	6,	1863	"
4083	Beer, Samuel	"							

DESCRIPTIVE LIST.

No.	Name	Rank	Co.	Regiment	Date	Year	Remarks
4089	Bucher, Henry	Private,	E	151 Infantry,	July 14,	1863	Frederick.
4093	Bancroft, A. J.	"	L	14 Cavalry,	May 11,	1864	"
4113	Bauchman, Levi	"	F	12 "	Aug. 6,	1864	"
4138	Bent, Thomas	"	H	5 "	Sept. 19,	1862	"
4146	Brandt, Charles	"		46 Infantry,	Oct. 4,	1862	"
4211	Baxter, David	"	D	72 "	Oct. 2,	1862	"
4203	Burton, Jered M.	Corporal,	A	107 "	Oct. 9,	1862	"
4197	Baker, M.	Private,		Teamster,	Dec. 27,	1862	"
4193	Berry, John S.	"	K	28 Infantry,	April 7,	1862	Age 32—Frederick. Cumberland.
4177	Beavers, Norman	"	L	Cavalry,			
4156	Boggs, Albert	"	D	1 "	Sept. 28,	1864	Clarysville.
4151	Bouch, Isaac	"	M	14 "	July 30,	1863	Antietam battlefield.
3611	Clark, Elwin	"	L	12 "			"
3641	Crick, J. W.	"		28 Infantry,			"
3662	Carr, Bernard	"		69 "			"
3672	Carpenter, George W.	"	G	111 "	Sept. 17,	1862	"
3676	Cole, Campbell	"	H	6 Inf. Reserves,	Sept. 17,	1862	"
3691	Clark, William	"	K	11 "	Sept. 17,	1862	"
3797	Crater, Jacob B.	"	H	3 "	Sept. 17,	1862	"
3784	Clark, Thomas H.	"	I	125 Infantry,	Sept. 17,	1862	"
3746	Carton, Peter	Corporal,		28 "	Sept. 17,	1862	"
3745	Costello, Charles	Private,	P	7 "	Sept. 22,	1862	"
3721	Church, Harry	"	H	136 "	Jan. 20,	1863	Smoketown.
3713	Clark, Joseph Z.	"	G	132 Inf. Reserves,	Sept. 17,	1862	"
3809	Cator, George H.	"	L	111 Infantry,	Oct. 15,	1862	"
3817	Clark, William H.	"	A	123 "	Nov. 4,	1862	Wounded Sept. 14, 1862. Smoketown. South Mountain.
3824	Callahan, Peter	"	K	1 "			"
3856	Canfield, Frederick	Corporal,	C	45 "			Middletown.
3882	Campbell, Jacob	Private,	A	45 "	May 5,	1864	Brownsville.
3888	Chambers, Henry	"	K	45 "	Sept. 12,	1864	Weverton.
3918	Chranister, John D.	"	E	12 Cavalry,	Oct. 18,	1862	Age 22—Removed from Frederick
4015	Clark, I. F.	"	M	47 Infantry,	Oct. 10,	1862	Removed from Frederick.
4006	Clouser, William H.	"	O	136 "	Oct. 10,	1862	"
3944	Costley, John	"	B	71 "	Oct. 24,	1862	"
3935	Carey, John	"	K	107 "			"
3934	Cauchlin, James	"	A	137 "			"
3929	Clendenan, G. Washington	"	D	134 "	Nov. 14,	1862	Age 35—Removed from Frederick.
4035	Clark, J. D.	"	H				

100   ANTIETAM NATIONAL CEMETERY.

PENNSYLVANIA—Continued.

Headst'e No.	NAME	Rank	Company	Regime't	Arm of Service	Date of Death	REMARKS
4036	Christie, Garn M.	Private,	F	134	Infantry,	Nov. 7, 1862	Age 27—Removed from Frederick.
4045	Campbell, John	"	K	155	"	Nov. 9, 1862	Age 21—Removed from Frederick.
4073	Caushey, Lebous B.	Sergeant,	C	4	Cavalry,	June 29, 1863	Removed from Frederick
4095	Cooper, Jere	Private,	K	12	"	July 12, 1864	Removed from Frederick
4090	Colter, Henry	"	A	138	Infantry,	July 14, 1864	Age 28. Removed from Frederick.
4120	Cohn, Uriah	"	M	12	Cavalry,	Oct. 12, 1864	Removed from Frederick.
4208	Crooks, J. W.	"	G	100	Infantry,	Oct. 4, 1862	Removed from Frederick.
4202	Clark, John	"	A	72	"	Oct. 6, 1862	Removed from Frederick.
4160	Chester, Samuel	"	K	112	"		Frostburg.
4158	Casey, James	"	B	84	"		Clarysville.
3583	Dowling, James	Corporal,	G	51	"	Sept. 17, 1862	Antietam battlefield.
3592	Dailey, Myers	Private,	A	53	"	Sept. 17, 1862	"
3593	Deagle, Gotleib	"	A	53	"	Sept. 17, 1862	"
3610	Dierfield, James H.	"	H	125	"		"
3616	Davis, J. C.	Sergeant,		51	"		"
3639	Dowda, R. O.	Private,		28	"		"
3643	Douglass, Edmund	Corporal,		72	"		"
3659	Daw, J.	Private,	D	111	"	Sept. 17, 1862	"
3660	Denney, William	"	I	111	"		"
3667	Davis, John E.	"			"		"
3786	Dowd, Thomas	"	D	106	"	Sept. 17, 1862	"
3811	Dougherty, Hugh	"	F	81	"	Oct. 17, 1862	"
3822	Daunt, William	"		4	Cavalry,		
3825	Dean, Henry W.	"	B	12	Inf. Reserves,		Middletown.
3911	Davis, Lewis	"	E	51	Infantry,		Weverton.
4005	Dreber, William	"	H	50	"	Oct. 17, 1862	Hagerstown.
3989	Dufford, Chronce	"	D	137	"	Nov. 4, 1862	"
3969	Davison, William	"	D	137	"	Dec. 5, 1862	Frederick.
4049	Dickson, William S.	"	K	9	"	Nov. 7, 1864	Age 35. Frederick.
4128	Doty, Nathaniel	"	E	102	"	June 10, 1864	Frederick.
4092	Duffy, J. H.	"	L	14	Cavalry,		

DESCRIPTIVE LIST.

	Name	Rank	Co.	Regt.	Arm	Enlisted		Remarks
3890	English, George	Private,	I	45	Infantry,	Nov. 12,	1862	South Mountain.
4034	Emery, Adam	"	E	134	"	Sept. 29,	1862	Frederick.
4207	Edwards, James	"	C	29	"	Mar. 10,	1862	Age 41—Frederick.
4187	Erhart, Nicholas	"	D	19	"	Oct. 23,	1862	Frederick.
3933	Eastman, Israel C.	"	G	87	"	Aug. 12,	1863	Antietam.
3622	Fries, Daniel D.	"	P	28	"			
3626	Flood, Edward	"	H	107	"	Sept. 17,	1862	
3736	Fesler, Samuel	"	D	111	"	Nov. 8,	1862	Smoketown.
3707	Fredenburgh, William	"	E	11	Inf. Reserves,	Sept. 14,	1862	South Mountain.
3847	Ferguson, Scott M.	"	F	1	"			"
3853	Fadden, Charles	Corporal,	G	45	Infantry,			
3879	Fenton, Henry	Private,	F	1	Inf. Reserves,			Middletown.
3904	Folger, Augustus	"	A	9	"			"
3909	Forrest, William E.	"	M	11	Cavalry,	Nov. 23,	1864	Weverton.
4011	Forrester, Archibald B.	"	B	139	Infantry,	Nov. 13,	1862	Age 20—Hagerstown.
3968	Fair, Chambers	"	I	139	"	Nov. 16,	1862	Age 18—Hagerstown.
3951	Fitzpatrick, Michael	"	F	23	"	Oct. 16,	1862	Age 23—Frederick.
3938	Fee, Samuel	"	G	123	"	Nov. 14,	1862	Age 19—Frederick.
4039	Fairly, Samuel	"	A	53	"	Nov. 27,	1862	Frederick.
4046	Fry, Isaac	"	G	49	"	Nov. 16,	1862	Hagerstown.
3957	Fawvor, J. H.	"	B	155	"	Oct. 6,	1862	Antietam battlefield.
3724	Fowles, Erred	"	C	129	"	Dec. 2,	1862	Frederick.
4048	Frederick, John	"	C	45	"	Mar. 18,	1863	Age 19—Frederick.
4079	Fields, James	"	K	158	"	Aug. 6,	1864	Frederick.
4106	Fluck, P. L.	"	F	12	Cavalry,	Aug. 3,	1864	Age 24—Frederick.
4107	Flemmer, Thomas	"	A	14	"	Aug. 12,	1864	Frederick.
4116	Fogg, Hosea	"	H	31	Infantry,	Sept. 23,	1862	
4141	Fox, William	"	D	1	Artillery	Mar. 19,	1865	Clarysville.
4172	Freeman, George W.	"	K	142	Infantry,	Oct. 28,	1862	Frederick.
3924	Fastnought, W. H.	"	B	107	"	Unknown,		Antietam battlefield.
3761	Fresler, G. C.	"	K	130	"	Sept. 17,	1862	"
3599	Good, Christian	"	C	134	"	Oct. 27,	1862	"
3618	Garvin, Milton	Corporal,	G	125	"	Sept. 17,	1862	"
3644	Gibbony, James H.	Private,	F	111	"	Sept. 17,	1862	"
3671	Graham, Robert M.	"	H	6	Inf. Reserves,			
3674	Gibberd, John	Corporal,		11	Inf. or Cav'y,			
3720	Galusha, Truman	Private,	F	8	Inf. Reserves,	Sept. 17,	1862	Smoketown
3717	Gates, James							

PENNSYLVANIA—Continued.

Headst'e No.	NAME	Rank	Company	Regiment	Arm of Service	Date of Death	REMARKS
3706	Griffith, Wesley	Private,	D	142	Infantry,	Dec. 16, 1862	Smoketown.
3855	Goodman, Charles	"	E	"	"	"	South Mountain.
3881	Glenn, J. H.	Corporal,	A	45	"	"	"
4028	Green, Scott W.	Private,	"	12	Cavalry,		Burkettsville.
3962	Graham, John	"	"	4	"	Oct. 4, 1861	3 months' service. Hagerstown.
3959	Godfrey, William C.	"					Hagerstown.
4038	George, William	"	G	134	Infantry,	Nov. 18, 1862	Age 35—Frederick.
4081	Gilbert, David	"	I	172	"	July 26, 1863	Age 18—Frederick.
4097	Griffith, John	"	M	12	Cavalry,	July 10, 1864	Frederick.
4136	Gehr, L. D.	"	E	111	Infantry,	Aug. 15, 1862	Age 20—Frederick,
4140	Grove, William P.	Lieut.	A	45	"	Sept. 23, 1862	Frederick,
4210	Gusten, H. C.	Private,	H	6	"	Oct. 3, 1862	"
4103	Galigher, F. H.	"	M	12	Cavalry,	July 10, 1864	"
4115	Green, J. C.	"	A	14	"	Aug. 12, 1863	"
4127	Ginter, Peter	"	F	17	"	Dec. 9, 1864	"
4130	Gilliland, John	"		169	Engineers,	June 3, 1865	"
4188	Gibson, Israel	"	B	111	Infantry,	July 16, 1862	"
4183	Gibbs, Mason	Corporal,	F	54	Cavalry,		Cumberland.
4173	Grim, Adam W.	Private,	K	14	Cavalry,	Nov. 13, 1864	Clarysville.
4157	Grambling, Solomon	"	L	54	Infantry,	June 1, 1864	"
4166	Hathfen, W. S.	"	G	1	"	Aug. 8, 1863	Oldtown.
3586	Hurst, William J.	Corporal,		50	"		Antietam battlefield.
3589	Heether, James	Private,	H	118	"	Sept. 17, 1862	"
3609	Hess, Samuel	"	P	125	"	"	"
3628	Hofinan, Gustavus	"	P	28	"	"	"
3627	Hart, Thomas	"		28	"	"	"
3640	Hughs, George	"	K	28	"	"	"
3657	Hand, John	"	H	69	Inf. Reserves,	Sept. 17, 1862	"
3677	Huck, William	"		6	Inf. Reserves,	Sept. 17, 1862	"
3682	Hangthiter, C. M.	"		72	Infantry,		"
3683	Huber, Edward	Corporal,	I	72	"	Sept. 17, 1862	"

DESCRIPTIVE LIST.

No.	Name	Rank	Co.	Regiment	Date	Year	Place
3765	Hetrick, James	Private,		72 Infantry,			
3752	Hamilton, James	"		28 "			Antietam battlefield.
3735	Hopkins, T. C.	"		11 Inf. or Cav'y.			"
3731	Haman, ———						
3723	Hallowell, John	"	A	51 Infantry,	Sept. 17,	1862	"
3722	Hollingsworth, George	Corporal,	C	4 Inf. Reserves,	Nov. 28,	1862	Thompson's Battery. Smoketown.
3711	Henderson, Thomas	Private,	B	"	Oct. 4,	1862	Smoketown.
3700	Hankins, George H.	"		"	Oct. 25,	1862	"
3821	Hunt, George	"	H	132 Infantry,	Oct. 12,	1862	Antietam.
3810	Harris, Robert	"	A	142 "	Sept. 14,	1862	South Mountain.
3871	Hunter, William	"	B	128 "	Sept. 14,	1862	"
3877	Hotchkiss, J. M.	"	D	45 "	Sept. 14,	1862	"
3878	Hurd, James	"	H	45 "	Sept. 17,	1862	Antietam battlefield.
3768	Horton, George	"	F	45 "			South Mountain.
3887	Holliday, M. G.	"		8 Inf. Reserves,			"
3903	Hill, Thomas	"		46 Infantry,			Middletown.
3917	Hennan, Joseph W.	"	H	5 Inf. Reserves,			
4019	Harland, John	"	E	100 Infantry,	Aug. 20,	1863	Burkettsville.
4002	Hoffacker, John	Corporal,	C	1 Artillery,			Weverton.
3991	Hathaway, Jesse	Private,	E	18 Cavalry,	Oct. 21,	1862	Hagerstown.
3976	Holloran, Michael	"	K	137 Infantry,	Sept. 26,	1862	"
3942	Heard, Thomas	"	K	96 "	Oct. 19,	1862	Age 42—Frederick.
3928	Hollingsworth, John	"	L	51 "	Oct. 27,	1862	Frederick.
3927	Hostetler, John J.	"		72 "	Oct. 24,	1862	"
4037	Hayes, William B.	"	B	107 "	Nov. 19,	1862	Age 20—Frederick.
4052	Hackenburg, J. W.	Sergeant,	K	155 "	Nov. 4,	1862	Age 43—Frederick.
4058	Herger, Michael	Private,	D	131 "	Nov. 17,	1862	Age 28—Frederick.
4076	Harrison, J. F.	"	D	129 "	June 29,	1863	Frederick.
4094	Hensler, Peter	"	I	115 "	Sept. 10,	1864	"
4168	Hartsell, George	"	M	20 Vet. Cavalry,	Sept. 10,	1864	"
4117	Hahn, Sidney	"	A	12 Cavalry,	Aug. 8,	1864	
4129	Hall, Volney F.	"	B	47 Infantry,	June 11,	1865	
4145	Harman, Henry	"		14 "	Oct. 3,	1862	
4201	Holden, Nicholas	"		12 Inf. Reserves,	Oct. 5,	1862	
4192	Hopkins, William H.	"	A	8 "	July 5,	1862	
4166	Halifen, W. S.	"	G	109 Infantry,	Aug. 8,	1863	Oldtown.
4155	Hawse, William N.	"	C	1 "	Sept. 23,	1864	Clarysville.
4151	Himes, W. W.	"	M	20 Cavalry,	June 3,	1864	
				22 "			

104   ANTIETAM NATIONAL CEMETERY.

PENNSYLVANIA—CONTINUED.

Headst'e No.	NAME	Rank	Company	Regiment	Arm of Service	Date of Death	REMARKS
4153	Hemming, Henry	Private,	I	54	Infantry,	April 22, 1864	Clarysville.
3995	Itle, John	"	M	12	Cavalry,	Sept. 3, 1864	Weverton.
3845	James, Thomas	"	G	11	Inf. Reserves,	Sept. 14, 1862	South Mountain.
3885	Jordan, Martin	"	M	100	Infantry,	" "	"
4027	James, George	"	L	96	"	Sept. 14, 1862	Burkettsville.
4016	Jackson, John	"	A	14	Cavalry,	May 10, 1864	Brownsville.
3961	Jackson, Thomas	"	M	18	"	" "	Hagerstown.
4077	Jeffries, Henry F.	"	I	53	Infantry,	Feb. 28, 1863	Age 24—Frederick.
4171	Johnson, William	"	B	20	Cavalry,	"	Cumberland.
4118	Jones, George	"	B	12	"	"	Frederick.
3981	Jewell, Zenas	Sergeant,	G	18	"	July 6, 1863	Hagerstown.
4062	Jones, William D.	Private,	I	130	Infantry.	Dec. 14, 1862	Frederick.
3651	Kunkle, Andrew	"	A	28	"	Sept. 17, 1862	Antietam battlefield.
3648	Kelly, Patrick	"		90	"	" "	"
3666	Keep, Alsinus	Corporal,	E	111	"	Sept. 17, 1862	"
3743	Kinney, George W.	Private,		12	Inf. Reserves,	"	Antiet'm battlefield. Wounded Sept. 17, 1862.
3742	Kreuson, Luther	"	F	3	"	"	" "
3741	Krum, William F.	"	G	152	Infantry,	"	"
3696	Kehoe, Thomas	"	C	107	"	Sept. 17, 1862	Smoketown.
3872	Kerr, Robert	"	C	45	"	"	South Mountain.
3893	Keplar, Jacob	"	K	45	"	"	"
3898	Kimberlin, John G.	"	B	11	Inf. Reserves,	"	"
4003	Kirkpatrick, James E.	Corporal,	H	22	Cavalry,	Aug. 4, 1864	Weverton.
3996	Kosier, Jesse	Private,	D	47	Infantry,	Oct. 31, 1864	
3975	Kirby, Patrick	"		5	Artillery,		Hagerstown.
3967	Kirkpatrick, John	"	D	137	Infantry,	Nov. 2, 1862	Age 18—Hagerstown.
3949	Kelly, Amer	"	D	102	"	Oct. 23, 1862	Age 44—Hagerstown.
3941	Kennedy, Partial	"	K	50	"	Oct. 18, "	Frederick.
4090	Kimble, Henry	"	A	171	"	July 20, 1863	Age 23—Frederick.
4126	Keller, Fidelle	"		87	"	Oct. 10, 1864	Frederick.
4194	Knipp, Philip	"	H	28	"	July 1, 1862	Age 21—Frederick.

DESCRIPTIVE LIST.

No.	Name	Rank	Co.	Regt.	Date	Year	Remarks
4190	Kinter, Montgomery	Private,	C,	111 Infantry,	July 10,	1862	Age 25—Frederick.
4047	Keister, A. L.	"	F,	28 "	Nov. 28,	1862	Frederick.
4050	Knoppenberger, Charles	"	N,	28 "	Dec. 1,	1862	"
4055	King, Stephen	"	D,	136 "	Dec. 6,	1862	Age 20—Frederick.
4067	Kaercher, James						
4105	Kugler, S. D.	"	F,	49 "	Aug. 6,	1864	Frederick.
4059	Kiles, Charles	"	B,	1 "	Dec. 1,	1862	"
3605	Layman, Ephraim	Corporal,	I,	118 "	Sept. 20,	1862	Antietam battle-field.
3634	Lier, John	Private,	E,	125 "	Sept. 17,	1862	"
3776	Leese, James	"	F,	3 Inf. Reserves,	Sept. 17,	1862	"
3738	Lord, D. R.						
3837	Laughery, William	"	B,	11 "	Sept. 14,	1862	South Mountain.
4032	Lightner, David						Middletown.
4007	Little, Augustus	"	G,	45 Infantry,	Oct. 18,	1864	Weverton.
3999	Lewis, Edward	"	D,	12 Cavalry,	Oct. 10,	1864	"
3984	Lord, Benjamin	"	K,	87 Infantry,	Oct. 31,	1862	Hagerstown.
3965	Logan, James	"	H,	137 "	Oct. 13,	1862	Age 27—Hagerstown.
3926	Lerch, John	"	B,	139 "	Oct. 22,	1862	Frederick.
4069	Loomis, Chamberlin	"	E,	9 "	Dec. 23,	1862	Age 21—Frederick.
4078	Linn, Henry	"	A,	134 "	Mar. 31,	1863	Age 25—Frederick.
4131	Lynch, John	"	L,	6 "	Feb. 15,	1865	Frederick.
4133	Lucas, Benjamin	"	L,	87 "	June 17,	1862	"
4165	Lydick, Daniel	"	G,	73 "			
4148	Law, James	"	C,	2 U. S. S. S.	Oct. 15,	1862	Six months' service. Oldtown.
4143	Loafman, William	Corporal,	H,	8 Infantry,	Sept. 25,	1862	Removed from Frederick.
3584	Moore, H. C.	Private,				1862	Frederick.
3594	Milligan, Jephtha	"	K,	51 "	Sept. 17,	1862	Antietam battlefield.
3600	Marshall, John	"	L,	132 "	Sept. 17,	1862	"
3603	McDermott, Thomas J.	"	I,	28 "	Sept. 24,	1862	"
3608	McCracken, Joseph	"	I,	118 "	Sept. 17,	1862	"
3613	McCarl, Edward	"	F,	125 "	July 17,	1863	"
3615	Marshall, James	"	E,	84 "	Sept. 17,	1862	"
3619	Mapp, James F.	"	K,	129 "	Oct. 23,	1862	"
3621	McMillan, Archibald	"	B,	155 "	Nov. 7,	1862	"
3625	Mullen, R. M.			28 "			Knapp's Battery.
4205	McTague, Patrick		I,	6 "			
3637	McCloskey, Thomas	Sergeant,	F,	28 "	Sept. 27,	1862	Frederick.
3649	Mason, Theodore	Private,		90 "	Sept. 17,	1862	Antietam battlefield.

PENNSYLVANIA—CONTINUED.

Hendal's No.	NAME.	Rank.	Company	Reg'ment	Arm of Service.	Date of Death.	REMARKS.
3651	Mitchell, Samuel	Private,	A	90	Infantry,		Antietam battlefield.
3655	Millhoff, Charles	"	E	88	"	Sept. 17, 1862	"
3668	Miller, Jacob N.	"		111	"	Sept. 17, 1862	"
3690	Mammoth, ——	Sergeant,	C	131	Inf. Reserves,	Oct. 16, 1862	"
3799	Mower, Jacob	Private,	E	2	Infantry,	Sept. 17, 1862	"
3791	McKechner, William	"	C	69	Inf. Reserves,	Sept. 17, 1862	"
3787	Moss, James	"		9	Infantry,	Sept. 17, 1862	"
3758	Mahaffey, Robert	Sergeant,	K	28	Inf. Reserves,	Sept. 17, 1862	"
3750	Madden, James	Private,	F	28	Infantry,	Sept. 17, 1862	"
3747	McMullen, Alexander J.	"		1	Inf. Reserves,		"
3730	Moore, T. S.	"	G	2	"	Nov. 28, 1862	Smoketown.
3719	Means, Henry W.	"		6	"	Sept. 17, 1862	"
3715	Murphy, Bernard	"		137	Infantry,	Nov. 5, 1862	"
3704	Martin, William H.	"	F	9	Inf. Reserves,	Oct. 9, 1862	"
3699	McCormick, David B.	"	E	142	Infantry,	Nov. 24, 1862	"
3697	Martin, Henry	"	K	106	"	Oct. 17, 1862	"
3695	McVey, John	"	F	8	Inf. Reserves,	Nov. 20, 1862	"
3814	Malone, William	"	I	1	"		South Mountain.
3851	Maxson, William M.	"			"		"
3861	Miller, George	"					"
3862	McKellar, Charles	"	C	100	Infantry,		"
3884	Miller, J. C.	"	F	100	"		"
3889	McClarren, George	"	K	45	Inf. Reserves,		Middletown.
3892	McCann, James	"		12	Infantry,		"
3913	Melott, Frederick	"	H	100	"		
3920	McLaughlin, John H.	"	D	96	"	Sept. 30, 1862	Burkettsville.
4031	Miller, Aaron	"	C	14	Cavalry,	May 7, 1864	Brownsville.
4014	McKeever, John	"	K	51	Infantry,		Weverton.
4001	Munsick, David	"		12	Cavalry,	June 17, 1864	Antietam.
3998	McCallen, Charles	"		50	Infantry,		
3978	McGlann, Daniel	"					

DESCRIPTIVE LIST.

No.	Name	Rank	Co.	Regiment	Date	Year	Remarks
3973	Mc——, ——	Private,	C	1 Artillery,	Nov. 7,	1862	Hagerstown.
3950	McKnight, James	1st Serg't,	G	51 Infantry,	Oct. 20,	1862	Frederick.
3943	Mercer, George	Private,	E	1 Inf. Reserves,	Oct. 16,	1862	"
3940	Mangold, Peter	"	C	83 Infantry,	Oct. 28,	1862	"
3925	Mundoff, John P.	"	H	"	Nov. 18,	1862	"
4042	McGuire, M. C.	"	K	128			
4044	Moore, Isaac L.	"	C	155	Nov. 15,	1862	Age 20—Frederick.
4056	McDevitt, Hugh	"	C	69	Dec. 10,	1862	Age 30—Frederick.
4063	McCracken, A. M.	"	G	145	Dec. 13,	1862	Age 30—Frederick.
4065	Marks, Joseph H.	"	G	6 Cavalry,	Jan. 6,	1863	Frederick.
4070	Miller, Jeremiah	"	H	69 Infantry,	Jan. 3,	1863	"
4071	Morse, David	"	A	11 "	Jan. 3,	1863	
4075	Morse, Joel F.	"	D	56 "	June 2,	1863	
4084	Miller, W. H.	"	B	172 "	July 21,	1863	Age 33—Frederick.
4104	McDaniel, Joseph	"	B	14 Cavalry,	July 11,	1864	Frederick.
4119	Moore, W. H.	"	L	4 "	Aug. 24,	1864	
4132	Miller, Samuel	"	D	104 Infantry,	Feb. 27,	1865	
4135	Monaghan, Hamilton	"	F	124 "	Sept. 23,	1862	
4142	Morton, Noah C.	"	L	45 "	Sept. 27,	1862	
4144	McCurdy, James	"	M	28 "	Sept. 24,	1862	
4195	McArthur, Thomas	"	P	28 "	Feb. 28,	1862	
4198	Moore, Joseph	"	G	28 "	Mar. 14,	1862	Age 21—Frederick.
4189	McNight, John	"	E	73 "	July 26,	1862	Age 34—Frederick.
4186	McGuigan, J. M.	"			Sept. 16,	1864	Independent Engineers. Frederick.
4182	Monaghan, Michael	"					Cumberland.
4170	Marsh, J. W.	"	L	22	Sept. 30,	1863	Six months' service. Oldtown.
3698	McCollins, John	"	C	2 Battery,	Oct. 8,	1862	Smoketown.
3823	McLaughlin, J.	"	C	2 Inf. Reserves,			Antietam.
3858	Moss, Charles	"	M	4 Cavalry,			
3921	Marchand, Nicholas	"	F	8 Inf. Reserves,	Sept. 14,	1862	South Mountain.
4109	Miricle, Henry	"	A	155 Infantry,	Nov. 19,	1862	Age 18—Frederick.
3645	Nace, Josiah	"	C	12 Cavalry,	Sept. 22,	1864	Frederick.
3785	Nourse, Thomas A.	Corporal,	D	90 Infantry,			Antietam battlefield.
3766	Noch, W. H. H.	Private,	E	6 Inf. Reserves,	Sept. 17,	1862	"
3748	Nuss, Jacob	"		72 Infantry,	Sept. 17,	1862	"
3734	Noal, John	"		28 "			
3899	Northrop, A. D.	"	L				South Mountain.
3955	Norton, David	"	M	1 Cavalry,			Hagerstown.

ANTIETAM NATIONAL CEMETERY.

PENNSYLVANIA—Continued.

Headst'e No.	Name	Rank	Company	Regiment	Arm of Service	Date of Death	Remarks
3930	Ness, Robert	Private,	H	9	Bucktail,	Oct. 26, 1862	Frederick.
4200	Newpher, James	"	L	1	Infantry,	Oct. 6, 1862	"
4178	Nesbit, James	"	E	110	Infantry,		Cumberland.
4161	Nedren, Jacob	"	D	22	Cavalry,	Oct. 17, 1864	Clarysville.
3780	Overdorff, David C.	"	H	12	Inf. Reserves,		Antietam.
3813	Otten, Henry	"	A	3	"	Oct. 12, 1862	Smoketown.
3886	Olenbaugh, H. C.	"	A	100	Infantry,		South Mountain.
3902	Otis, James	"			Nevin's Bat'y,	Unknown,	Middletown.
3550	Phillips, Samuel	"		118	Infantry,		Antietam.
3617	Pickering, Joseph J.	"	D	90	"	Sept. 17, 1862	"
3670	Ploss, Wheeler	"		111	"	Sept. 17, 1862	"
3658	Parker, John A.	"		28	"		"
3642	Penn, George	"		28	"		South Mountain.
3840	Price, Abraham	"	E	45	"		"
3874	Parsons, Thomas	"	C	12	Cavalry,	Nov. 11, 1864	Weverton.
4008	Proctor, George F.	"	L	49	Infantry,	Oct. 7, 1862	"
3992	Price, F. H.	"	D	139	"	Nov. 7, 1864	Age 36—Hagerstown.
3952	Pardoe, R. J.	Sergeant,	A	14	Cavalry,	July 7, 1864	Frederick.
4096	Pattison, T. M.	Private,	K	87	Infantry,	Jan. 5, 1865	"
4123	Perry, Timothy	"	H	124	"	Sept. 30, 1862	"
4214	Paiste, William H.	"	H	8	"	Oct. 3, 1863	"
4212	Peters, John	"	F	110	"	Unknown,	Cumberland.
4179	Paulus, Samuel	"	C	14	Cavalry,	May 2, 1865	Clarysville
4159	Pohl, Frederick	"	A	28	Infantry,	Sept. 17, 1862	Antietam battlefield.
3632	Quinn, Patrick	"	K	2	Inf. Reserves,	Oct. 1862	Smoketown.
3710	Quinn, James F.	"		134	Infantry,		Antietam battlefield.
3607	Rancy,	"	A	134	"	Oct. 10, 1862	"
3623	Rudesill, Musser J.	"	D	28	"	Sept. 17, 1862	"
3629	Ritter, George J.	"	C	28	"	Sept. 17, 1862	"
3630	Reynolds, Emmor	"		78	"	Sept. 17, 1862	"
3678	Rever, Jacob	"	L	72	"		"

DESCRIPTIVE LIST.

No.	Name	Rank	Co.	Reg.	Arm	Date	Year	Remarks
3788	Reedy, Michael	Private,	C	69	Infantry,	Sept. 17,	1862	Antietam battlefield.
3760	Reiff, Jacob	"	"	9	Inf. Reserves,	Sept. 17,	1862	"
3728	Richey, W. C.	"	"	"	"	"	"	"
3712	Job, Rohn	"	D	11	Inf. or Cav'y.	Nov. 19,	1862	Smoketown.
3701	Rice, Jacob	"	E	106	Infantry,	Oct. 14,	1862	"
3910	Roberts, Peter	"	"	"	"			Middletown.
3915	Ray, Madison	"	"	"	"			"
4013	Randall, J. H.	"	K	12	Cavalry,			Brownsville.
3994	R——, John J.	"	"	"	"			Weverton.
3974	Rifenberger, H. H.	"	"	146	Infantry.		1861	Hagerstown.
3947	Rowland, William	"	D	3	"	Nov. 4,	1862	Age 32—Fredrick.
4051	Rudy, J. P.	"	G	129	"	Dec. 7,	1862	Age 18—Frederick.
4054	Reed, J. C.	"	D	134	"	June 29,	1863	Frederick.
4074	Rager, David	"	A	115	"	July 20,	1864	Age 21—Frederick.
4111	Rodenbaugh, William	"	A	38	"			Cumberland.
4184	Reinninger, Frederick M.	"	K	84	"	Aug. 8,	1863	Clarysville.
4150	Romig, Franklin	"	F	54	"			Antietam battlefield.
3582	Shultz, Henry	"	"	51	"			"
3597	Smith, John H.	"	B	132	"	Sept. 17,	1862	"
3604	Schmit, Frederick	"	D	118	"	"	"	"
3624	Sellers, Samuel	"	A	50	"			"
3658	Scullen, Patrick	"	"	106	"	Sept. 17,	1862	"
3679	Shoemaker, William	"	"	72	"	"	"	"
3592	Stevens, W. H.	"	C	124	"	Sept. 17,	1862	"
3798	Snodgrass, James L.	"	F	155	"	Nov. 16,	1862	"
3790	Shanefelt, James	"	"	11	Inf. or Cav'y,			
3759	Swartzlander, Adam	"	"	9	Inf. Reserves,	Sept. 17,	1862	"
3744	Spahr, David	"	"	7	Infantry.			
3729	Sanford, ——	"	F	50	"	Sept. 17,	1862	"
3726	Schermitzanner, Florance	"	B	45	"	"	"	"
3725	Spotts, Philips B.	"	G	28	"			
3702	Sherman, Moses	"	C	12	Cavalry,	Oct. 5,	1862	Removed from Smoketown.
3819	Stiles, George W.	"	"	8	Cav. Reserves.			Removed from Antietam battlefield.
3829	Struble, Henry	"	"	11	Inf. Reserves,	Sept. 14,	1862	Removed from Burkettsville.
3833	Stewart, Samuel T.	Sergeant,	G	11	"	"	"	"
3834	Schmidt, Charles	Private,	C	11	"	"	"	"
3835	Stuchell, Henry	"	B	11	"	Sept. 14,	1862	"
3836	Saxton, Charles A.	"	"	9	"			

ANTIETAM NATIONAL CEMETERY.

PENNSYLVANIA—CONTINUED.

Headst's No.	NAME.	Rank.	Company	Reg'ment	Arm of Service.	Date of Death.	REMARKS.
3846	S——, V.	Private,	G	11	Inf. Reserves,		Weverton.
3848	Sarver, Labanah	"	E	11	"		"
3854	Sweet, C. H.	"		1	"		"
3860	Simpson, ——	"			"		"
3864	Strump, Charles	"	G	5	Infantry,		"
3876	Squires, Jacob	"	B	6	Inf. Reserves,	Sept. 14, 1862	"
3907	Shell, David	"			"		"
3912	Stodden, P. E.	"			"		"
4009	Stall, William	"	E	20	Cavalry,	May 13, 1864	"
4004	Supplee, Robert	"	A	51	Infantry,		"
3990	Sherman, Ira	"		14	Cavalry,		Hagerstown.
3987	Smith, Andrew W.	"		14	"		"
3983	Snow, John S.	"	D	137	Infantry,	Oct. 19, 1862	"
3774	Spencer, C. J.	Corporal,		12	Inf. Reserves,	Unknown,	Antietam battlefield.
3977	Swank, Daniel	Private,	A	28	Infantry,	Oct. 16, 1861	Hagerstown.
3969	Shelby, Joseph	"	E	93	"	Sept. 28, 1862	Age 21—Hagerstown.
3964	Sutliff, David L.	"	I	84	"	Aug. 14, 1863	Hagerstown.
3963	Smith, William	"			"		"
3953	Simpson, George A.	"	B	125	"	Sept. 17, 1862	Age 22—Hagerstown.
3931	Smith, Philip	"	K	145	"	Oct. 23, 1862	Frederick.
3922	Smith, James A.	"	K	131	"	Nov. 19, 1862	"
4053	Schrecengost, Simon	Corporal,	C	155	"	Dec. 7, 1862	Age 32—Frederick.
4057	Shannon, Anderson	Private,	F	134	"	Nov. 5, 1862	Age 21—Frederick.
4060	Shreve, William	"		145	"	Dec. 19, 1862	Frederick.
4072	Smith, Valentine	"		8	Inf. Reserves,		South Mountain.
4080	Steinmetz, W. H.	"	A	71	Infantry,	April 3, 1863	Age 23—Frederick.
4085	Seibert, Jacob	"	I	149	"	Aug. 8, 1863	Age 27—Frederick.
4088	Spriggle, Benjamin	"	L	17	"	Aug. 12, 1863	Age 19—Frederick.
4091	Seybold, David	"	M	17	Cavalry,	July 18, 1863	Age 29—Frederick.
4102	Shedrone, Peter	"	H	22	"	July 11, 1864	Frederick.
4114	Showalter, M.	"	F	195	Infantry,	Aug. 27, 1864	Age 19—Frederick.

DESCRIPTIVE LIST.

No.	Name	Rank	Co.	Regt.	Date	Year	Remarks
4121	Snow, S. C.	Private,	L	11 Cavalry,	Jan. 4,	1865	Frederick.
4122	Shultz, C. W.	Corporal,	E	87 Infantry,	Oct. 12,	1864	"
4125	Speel, Henry	Private,	H	98 "	Jan. 7,	1865	"
4137	Seyfert, John	"	C	109 "	Aug. 22,	1862	"
4213	Shafer, Charles	"	I	109 "	Oct. 2,	1862	"
4209	Smith, Robert R.	"	H	28 "	Oct. 1,	1862	"
4206	Stevens, Jacob	"	C	11 "	Sept. 27,	1862	"
4191	Switzer, John	"		74 "	July 12,	1862	"
4185	Sullivan, Jeremiah	"					Elk County, Pennsylvania.
4180	Stout, Peter	"	E	18 "			Removed from Clarysville.
4176	Sullivan, William	"	G	110 "			Removed from Cumberland.
4174	Sell, William H.	"	K	14 Cavalry,	Aug. 17,	1864	Removed from Clarysville.
4152	Schellhorn, John	"	K	74 Infantry,	Apr. 30,	1865	Age 40—Clarysville.
3595	Teneyck, John H.	"	B	132 "	Sept. 17,	1862	Antietam battlefield.
3635	Taylor, I. S.	"		11 "			"
3652	Treon, Franklin	"	C	16 Cavalry,			"
3656	Tyson, Jesse	"	I	88 Infantry,	Sept. 17,	1862	"
3675	Taylor, R. B.	Corporal,		77 or 11 "			
3697	Tyler, John	Private,	F	12 Inf. Reserves,	Sept. 17,	1862	
3708	Ticknor, William	"	D	90 Infantry,	Nov. 15,	1862	Removed from Smoketown.
3818	Townsend, G. W.	"					Removed from Antietam battlefield.
3850	Troup, Simon	"	B	6 Inf. Reserves,	Oct. 1,	1862	Removed from South Mountain.
3868	Trask, A. A.	Sergeant,					Removed from South Mountain.
3894	Tremain, J. R.	Private,	H	45 Infantry,			Removed from South Mountain.
3958	Timbers, Charles	"	E	44 "	July 30,	1863	Removed from Hagerstown.
3923	Thompson, William	"	L	123 "	Nov. 11,	1862	Age 21—Frederick.
4061	Thompson, William	"	G	96 "	Dec. 18,	1862	Frederick.
4085	Taylor, James	"	H	8 "	Aug. 13,	1863	"
4100	Thompson, W. F.	"	L	27 Cavalry,	July 12,	1864	"
4134	Taylor, William C.	"	B	28 Infantry,	July 19,	1852	"
4043	Teats, J. A.	"	B	125 "	Nov. 30,	1862	"
3914	Ulrich, John	"	E	45 "			Burkettsville.
3650	Venable, Charles	"	F	90 "	Sept. 17,	1862	Antietam battlefield.
3680	Vaughan, Beverly K.	"	B	69 "			"
3727	Von Send, Andrew	"	B	9 Inf. Reserves,			"
4181	Vermillion, Helfrey	"	E	39 Infantry,			Hancock.
4149	Vantesson, Robert	"	E	12 Cavalry,	Mar. 4,	1864	Clarysville
3597	Watson, Samuel	"		118 Infantry,			Antietam battlefield.

PENNSYLVANIA—CONTINUED.

Hendst'e No.	NAME.	Rank.	Company	Regiment	Arm of Service.	Date of Death.	REMARKS.
3591	White, A. J.	Private,	D	53	Infantry,	Sept. 17, 1862	Antietam battlefield.
3596	Warner, George W.	Sergeant,	B	132	"	Sept. 17, 1862	"
3606	Wilson, J. G.	Private,	A	118	"	Sept. 20, 1862	"
3614	Wells, C. B.	"		72	"		"
3633	Wonderly, Charles H.	"	C	28	"	Sept. 17, 1862	"
3646	Waters, Alex	"		90	"		"
3654	Wilcox, George A.	"	A	16	Cavalry,		"
3669	Womer, Andrew	Corporal,	A	125	Infantry,	Sept. 17, 1862	"
4147	White, _____				Unknown,		Rem'd f'm Methodist gravey'd. June 11, 1872.
3800	White, Learies	Private,	B	123	Infantry,	Oct. 19, 1862	Antietam battlefield.
3781	Woodward, John	"	D	8	Inf. Reserves,	Sept. 17, 1862	"
3777	Wilson, Richard	"		3	"		"
3751	White, Harrison	"	B	28	Infantry,	Sept. 17, 1862	"
3749	Ward, Frederick C.	"	K	125	"	Sept. 17, 1862	"
3703	Wessner, Charles	"	K	96	"	Mar. 5, 1863	"
3816	Winder, Joseph	"	C	107	"	Oct. 19	"
3870	Walton, Amos	"	B	45	"		Smoketown.
3875	Wagner, Frank	"	J	45	"		South Mountain.
3901	Wilcox, Hiram	"	G	45	"		"
3916	Wells, Peter	Sergeant,	K	5	Inf. Reserves,		Middletown.
4022	Weaklam, W am	Private,		96	Infantry,		Burkettsville.
4017	Waters, George	"		20	Cavalry,		Brownsville.
4010	Wise, William	"	F	51	Infantry,		Weverton.
4000	Wilt, Joseph	"	F	22	Cavalry,	Sept. 14, 1864	"
3972	Wirt, E. H.	Corporal,	D	125	Infantry.		Hagerstown.
3939	Workmeister, George	Private,	E	90	"	Oct. 18, 1862	Frederick.
4087	Westworth, J.	Sergeant,	H	1	Cavalry,	Jan. 17, 1863	"
4098	Woolf, Anthony	Private,	C	27	Infantry,	July 11, 1864	"
4110	Waltemeyer, H. J.	"	O	89	"	Sept. 10, 1864	"
4199	Weaver, J. B.	"	B	28	"	Feb. 25, 1862	"
4175	Weaver, Joseph			6			Cumberland.

DESCRIPTIVE LIST 113

4168	Wilson, Charles	Private,					Oldtown.
4162	Wetherholt, George	"	C	22 Cavalry,	Sept. 29,	1864	Clarysville.
4101	Wiltinger, A.	"	A	27 "	July 13,	1864	Frederick.
4082	Yates, Alex.	"	A	18 Infantry,	July 25,	1863	Age 20—Removed from Frederick.
4139	Yarnell, Reuben	"	F	45 "	Sept. 21,	1862	Frederick.
4204	Basworth, Joseph T.	Private,	K	46 "	Dec. 26,	1861	Age 19—Removed from Frederick.
92	Unknown—Pennsylvania.						Removed from Antietam battlefield, South Mountain, Middletown, Burkettsville, Weverton and Hagerstown, Md

RHODE ISLAND.

2836	Abbott, Abiel J. N.	Private,	H	4 Infantry,	Sept. 17,	1862	Died of wounds Ant'tam. Rem'd f'm Ant'm.
2822	Burdick, Stephen H.	"	B	4 "	Sept. 17,	1862	Killed at Antietam. Rem'd from Antietam.
2823	Bantas, Gibbon	"		4 "	Sept. 17,	1862	"
2828	Burdick, Benjamin F.	Corporal,	D	1 Artillery	Sept. 17,	1862	"
2834	Basworth, Joseph T.	Private,	A	4 Infantry,	Sept. 17,	1862	"
2824	Fish, Henry	"	G	1 Light Artillery	Sept. 17,	1862	"
2858	French, Joseph S.	"	D	2 Infantry,	Oct. 24,	1862	Died at Smoket'wn. Rem'd f'm Smoket'wn.
2840	Fay, Michael	"	A	4 "			Age 38—Removed from Antietam battlefield.
2827	Hardy, John	"	D	4 "	Sept. 17,	1862	Killed at Antietam.
2842	Harvey, Samuel	Corporal,	B	4 "	June 11,	1863	Age 30—Removed from Frederick.
2889	Kent, C. B.	Sergeant,	C	2 "	July 25,	1863	Age 23—Removed from Frederick.
2829	Moon, Josiah	Private,	B	4 "	Sept. 17,	1862	Killed at Antietam. Rem'd from Antietam.
2831	McGowen, William	"	C	4 "	Sept. 17,	1862	"
2832	McNeal, Patrick	"	B	4 "	Sept. 17,	1862	"
2839	Manchester, Thomas	"	F	4 "	Nov. 23,	1862	Removed from Smoketown, Md.
2826	Stacey, Michael E.	"	C	4 "	Sept. 17,	1862	Killed at Antietam. Rem'd from Antietam.
2830	Suhager, Robert		A	1 Light Artillery			"
2833	Stone, Edward	"	E	4 Infantry,	Oct. 13,	1862	Removed from Antietam.
2837	Tyler, Edwin						
2821	Wilcox, Williard	Corporal,	B	4 "	Sept. 17,	1862	Killed at Antietam. Rem'd from Antietam.
2825	Weaver, Benoni	Private,	K	4 "	Sept. 17,	1862	Removed from Frederick.
2841	Wood, George	"	F	4 "			Removed from Antietam.
1	Unknown—Rhode Island.						

ANTIETAM NATIONAL CEMETERY.

WEST VIRGINIA.

Headst'e No.	NAME.	Rank.	Company	Regime't	Arm of Service.	Date of Death.	REMARKS.
2719	Ambrose, Marcus T.	Private,	G	13		Sept. 2, 1864	Removed from Weverton.
2721	Adkins, William S.	"	L	7	Cavalry,		"
2776	Ault, Henry	"	F	5	Cavalry,	Aug. 9, 1864	Removed from Cumberland.
2625	Barter, J. M.	"	D	9	Infantry.	Nov. 8, 1864	Removed from Frederick.
2734	Boothe, James S.	"	K	15	"	Aug. 26, 1864	Removed from Weverton.
2622	Bell, Robert	"	L	"	"	Sept. 16, 1864	Removed from Frederick.
2617	Brooks, George	"	H	9	Cavalry,	Sept. 24, 1862	"
2703	Bramhall, Sidney	"	K	3	Infantry.	Aug. 24, 1864	Age 28—Removed from Weverton.
2709	Ball, Jabez B.	"	A	1	Artillery,		Removed from Weverton.
2710	Brumage, Allen E.	"	E	13	Infantry,	April 28, 1865	"
2953	Burns, Benjamin	"	G	9	"	Aug. 27, 1864	"
2728	Burkhamer, George W.	"	F	1	Cavalry,	Mar. 24, 1862	Removed from Cumberland.
2773	Beerman, Daniel	"	G	10	Infantry,	Jan. 27, 1863	"
2772	Black, Hanson	"	D	1	Cavalry,	Feb. 1862	"
2850	Bates, Benjamin	"	D	14	Infantry,	Dec. 11, 1862	Died in Hospital, Cumberland, Md.
2859	Bird, George W.	"	D	1	"	July 22, 1862	Removed from Clarysville.
2861	Bone, William D.	"	C	"	"	July 29, 1864	"
2864	Brown, John	"	D	9	Cavalry,	June 5, 1864	"
2879	Bolyard, Josiah	"	D	13	Infantry,	Apr. 4, 1865	"
2873	Brooks, Andrew J.	"	D	10	"	Nov. 25, 1864	"
2944	Barnett, Thomas	"	K	13	"	Aug. 6, 1864	"
2948	Burrows, David	"	F	13	"	April 28, 1865	"
2716	Burns, Benjamin	"	E	10	"		"
2747	Brazell, Winfield S.	Corporal,	C	7		Nov. 6, 1862	Removed from Cumberland.
2630	Conway, Joseph W.	Private,	E	9		Sept. 26, 1864	Removed from Frederick.
2618	Cobb, James	"	G	1		July 10, 1864	Removed from Weverton.
2602	Cumpson, Thomas	"	C	9			Removed from Frederick.
2698	Cole, W. H.	"	B	1		Jan. 8, 1865	Removed from Weverton.
2711	Chedister, John	"		15	Cavalry,	Oct. 4, 1864	"
2715	Cunningham, J. Franklin	"	E	3		Aug. 25, 1864	Removed from Cumberland.
2720	Coats, William	"	F	15	Infantry.		

DESCRIPTIVE LIST.

No.	Name	Rank	Co.	Regt.	Arm	Date	Year	Remarks
2725	Castle, James L.	Private,	F	13	Infantry,	Aug. 12,	1864	Removed from Weverton. *
2770	Casto, Simon	"	E	1	Artillery,	July 31,	1863	Removed from Hancock.
2754	Cox, William L.	"	E	14	Infantry,	Dec. 26,	1862	Removed from Cumberland.
2943	Cochran, James F.	Corporal,	M	3	Cavalry,	Sept. 19,	1864	Removed from Clarysville
2950	Canterberry, Griffin	Private,	G	3	"	Apr.	1865	"
2951	Cozad, W. H. H.	Corporal,	L	6	Infantry,	Oct. 8,	1864	"
2955	Cunningham, William A.	Private,	A	10	"	July 6,	1864	Removed from Weverton. †
2620	Dodson, Charles G.	"	C	13	"	Aug. 31,	1864	Removed from Frederick.
2700	Drake, Guy F.	"	G	3	Cavalry,	Mar. 21,	1865	"
2704	De La Grange, Omie	"	C	1	"	July 17,	1862	Removed from Hancock.
2769	Dearman, Elliot	"	F	11	Infantry,	Sept. 5,	1863	Removed from Cumberland.
2761	Dakin, William G.	"	C	6	"	July 13,	1864	"
2849	Deyarman, John	"	F	7	"	Feb. 12,	1862	Removed from Weverton
2726	Douglass, Andrew J.	"	B	14	"	Aug. 27,	1864	Removed from Cumberland.
2854	Dye, John W.	"	D	14	"	Dec. 7,	1862	Removed from Clarysville.
2881	Durbin, David H.	"	F	7	"	May 20,	1862	"
2629	Elsey, Joshua	"	A	7	Cavalry,	Nov. 9,	1862	Removed from Frederick.
2615	Elderkin, Jackson	"	G	2	Infantry,	Nov. 9,	1864	"
2852	Edwards, Hamilton	"	G	10	"	April 23,	1862	Removed from Cumberland.
2863	Elmer, Frederick	"	H	15	"	Nov. 19,	1862	Removed from Clarysville.
2874	Edens, John	"	A	13	"	May 8,	1865	Removed from Clarysville.
2621	Felix, Warner	"	H	9	"	Sept. 4,	1864	Removed from Frederick.
2699	Furr, Abraham	"	H	10	"	Mar. 22,	1865	"
2707	Fox, William	"	D	1	"	April 29,	1862	"
2741	Farrell, Ias	"	H	4	"	Dec. 26,	1864	Removed from Clarysville.
2857	Fleming, Lewis G.	Sergeant,	C	11	"	Aug. 25,	1864	
2860	Faidlley, John	Private,	L	13	"	Nov. 29,	1862	
2886	Farmer, Thomas	"	E	15	"	Jan. 25,	1865	
2877	Farlin, Burwell	"	C	13	"	Mar. 17,	1865	
2952	Field, Benjamin F.	Corporal,	C	6	Cavalry,	July 18,	1864	
2628	Glass, James	Private,	F	5	Infantry,	Mar. 17,	1864	Removed from Frederick.
2609	Grove, George W.	"	D	7	"	Sept. 17,	1862	Removed from Antietam battlefield.
2614	Gallaher, Crawford	"	H	11	"	Dec. 25,	1864	Removed from Frederick.
2612	Goldsmith, William R.	"	B	9	"	Sept. 28,	1864	
2604	Gregory, James W.	"	K	7	"	Sept. 17,	1862	Removed from Smoketown.
2768	Gray, Henry A.	"	L	15	"	Dec. 3,	1862	Removed from Cumberland.
2746	Gould, Henry	"	F	7	"	Mar. 11,	1862	Removed from Cumberland.

* Supposed to be James L. Caster, Co. E, 15th Infantry, who died at Sandy Hook, August, 1864.　† Died from wounds received at Harper's Ferry, Va.

116   ANTIETAM NATIONAL CEMETERY.

WEST VIRGINIA—Continued.

Headst'e No.	NAME.	Rank.	Company	Regiment.	Arm of Service.	Date of Death.		REMARKS.
2736	Gillespie, Theophilus	Private,	A	13	Infantry.	Feb.	8, 1865	Removed from Clarysville.
2853	Grog, Joseph	"	G	10	"	Jan.	15, 1863	Removed from Cumberland.
2887	Green, John	"	A	13	"	Feb.	10, 1865	Removed from Clarysville.
2147	Greathouse, Richard	"	B	9	"	Aug.	1, 1864	Removed from Clarysville.
2631	Hannon, John N.	"	F	7	"	Nov.	29, 1862	Removed from Frederick.
2526	Hawkinberry, C.	"	G	15	"	Aug.	5, 1864	Removed from Frederick.
2603	Hulbert, James	"	G	10	"	July	7, 1864	Removed from Antietam battlefield.
2600	Harvey, William F. L.	Corporal,	H	12	"	Sept.	4, 1864	Removed from Weverton.
2712	Hostutler, Mark	Private,	A	9	"	Aug.	2, 1864	"
2777	Hansley, William	Corporal,	G	1	Cavalry,	July	27, 1865	Removed from Clarysville.
2764	Harman, Henry	"	F	14	Infantry,	Mar.	15, 1862	Removed from Cumberland.
2757	Hays, Abraham L.	"	E	"	"	Dec.	29, 1862	"
2742	Hamilton, Benjamin	"	C	9	"	Aug.	3, 1864	Removed from Clarysville.
2738	Hammock, Martin V. B.	Private,	L	11	"	July	23, 1864	"
2848	Hill, Henry	"	E	9	"	Dec.	14, 1862	Removed from Cumberland.
2883	Horton, James H.	"	G	11	"	Nov.	21, 1864	Removed from Clarysville.
2880	Harper, Peter W.	"	A	10	"	Dec.	17, 1864	"
2758	Jones, Samuel	"	A	13	"	May	12, 1865	Removed from Cumberland.
2752	Jones, John	"	F	7	"	Feb.	28, 1863	"
2606	Kent, George W.	Corporal,	F	7	"	Nov.	17, 1862	Removed from Smoketown.
2851	King, J. A.	Private,	F	7	"	April	23, 1862	Removed from Cumberland.
2856	Kiger, John	"	H	15	"	Dec.	20, 1862	"
2723	Layman, John J.	"	F	12	"	Sept.	15, 1864	Removed from Weverton.
2942	Lambert, John	"	K	1	"	Mar.	25, 1865	Removed from Clarysville.
2619	McClary, William	"	A	15	"	Sept.	16, 1864	Removed from Frederick.
2610	Myers, John M.	"	B	7	"	Feb.	5, 1862	Removed from Antietam battlefield.
2701	Mercer, Levi J.	"	C	2	"	April	9, 1865	Removed from Frederick.
2702	McDaniel, Milton	Corporal,	K	3	Cavalry,	Mar.	15, 1865	"
2706	Mallow, Isaac	Private,	I	7	Infantry,	Sept.	22, 1862	"
2708	McFarlane, Johnson	"	C	"	"	May	14, 1862	"
2774	Manning, Abraham	"	D	4	"	Mar.	17, 1865	Removed from Clarysville.

DESCRIPTIVE LIST.

	Name	Rank	Co.	Regt.	Arm	Date	Year	Remarks
2767	Moore, William	Private,	K	14	Infantry,	Aug. 4,	1864	Removed from Cumberland.
2763	McConnolley, William	"	D	12	"	"	"	"
2762	Meadows, John A.	"	F	10	"	Dec. 14,	1862	"
2755	Murry, Melvin	"	E	4	"	Dec. 24,	1864	"
2745	Mayley, Spencer	"	G	14	"	Sept. 4,	1863	"
2744	Marsh, Moses	"	D	14	"	Jan. 22,	1863	"
2846	Moore, Franklin	"	L	15	"	Feb. 20,	1863	"
2870	Morrow, William T.	Corporal,	F	1	Cavalry,	Aug. 25,	1864	Removed from Clarysville.
2868	McConnell, James	"	G	2	"	July 23,	1864	"
2867	Mossgrove, George V.	Sergeant,	L	1	"	Sept. 20,	1864	"
2866	Miller, William	Private,	E	6	Infantry,	Aug. 20,	1864	"
2940	Massie, Harvey	"	H	9	"	Aug. 24,	1864	Removed from Weverton.
2724	McMasters, George	"	K	14	"	Dec. 29,	1862	Removed from Cumberland.
2765	Norfolk, William	"	A	15	"	"	"	"
2844	Nagle, George	"	C	2	"	May 11,	1862	Removed from Oakland.
2871	Noon, Thomas	"	G	1	"	Sept. 16,	1864	Removed from Frederick.
2623	Pack, Newton R.	"	F	5	"	Oct. 3,	1864	Removed from Weverton.
2722	Piles, Isaac	"	A	1	Artillery,	Aug. 11,	1864	Age 19—Removed from Weverton.
2732	Provo, George	"	D	13	Infantry,	Sept. 27,	1864	Removed from Clarysville.
2869	Pickett, James D.	"	H	11	"	Mar. 7,	1865	Removed from Frederick.
2705	Rexroad, Loftus	"	F	3	Cavalry,	Aug. 24,	1864	Removed from Weverton.
2714	Roberts, William	"	G	10	Infantry,	Oct. 18,	1864	Age 29—Removed from Weverton.
2735	Ripley, Levi D.	"	E	10	"	May 12,	1865	Removed from Clarysville.
2775	Resling, J. C.	"	M	3	Cavalry,	Jan. 15,	1864	Removed from Cumberland.
2771	Riddle, James F.	"	G	10	Infantry,	Dec. 3,	1862	"
2760	Robinson, Edward S.	"	E	12	"	Dec. 24,	1862	"
2756	Roby, John	"	A	10	"	Feb. 20,	1865	"
2743	Robison, Mark E.	"	E	13	"	May 26,	1865	Removed from Clarysville.
2878	Rhoads, Peter M.	"	B	13	"	April 7,	1864	"
2865	Reader, John	"	K	5	Cavalry,	Aug. 24,	1863	Removed from Frederick.
2954	Roberts, Johnsey	"	A	9	Infantry,	July 4,	1862	Removed from Antietam battlefield.
2632	Stuber, Adam	"	C	1	Artillery	Sept. 17,	1862	"
2608	Shepherd, Hezekiah	"	D	7	Infantry	Oct. 4,	1862	Removed from Smoketown.
2607	Stafford, Solomon	"	E	"	"	Nov. 5,	1864	Removed from Weverton.
2605	Shell, John S.	"	L	7	"	Aug. 29,	1864	Mean's Loudoun Rangers.
2601	Stewart, Ephraim	"	B	7	"	Mar. 18,	1864	Removed from Weverton.
2730	Shackelford, James	"	A	13	Cavalry,	Sept.		
2731	Sowards, William W.	"	G	13	Infantry.			

118 ANTIETAM NATIONAL CEMETERY.

WEST VIRGINIA—CONTINUED.

Headst'e No.	NAME	Rank	Company	Regiment	Arm of Service	Date of Death	REMARKS
2717	Selby, Meredith	Private	G	3	Cavalry	Jan. 18, 1865	Removed from Weverton.
2733	Scott, Joseph	"	I	12	Infantry	July 30, 1864	"
2766	Stewart, Gerard	"		1	"		Removed from Cumberland.
2751	Short, Peter	"	B	9	"		"
2750	Shumate, C.	"		1	Cavalry		"
2749	Swisher, James W.	"	E	1	Light Artillery	July 23, 1863	Removed from Hancock.
2740	Six, Isaac	"	K	14	Infantry	Aug. 14, 1864	Removed from Clarysville.
2739	Snyder, David	"	H	15	"	July 19, 1864	"
2737	Sharp, Jeremiah F.	"	E	5	Cavalry	July 24, 1864	"
2843	Stoyer, William	"	C	6	Infantry	May 21, 1864	Removed from Cumberland.
2858	Short, James H.	"	C	10	"	1862	"
2945	Sargeant, William D.	Corporal	E	9	"	Aug. 18, 1864	Removed from Clarysville.
2753	Truman, Robert T.	Private	B	12	"	Dec. 14, 1862	Removed from Cumberland.
2862	Truman, Samuel	"	I	1	Battery	Feb. 14, 1865	Removed from Clarysville.
2885	Truslow, James	"	I	13	Infantry	April 6, 1865	"
2882	Thorn, Henry C.	"	I	14	"	Aug. 12, 1864	"
2611	2 Unknown,			7			Removed from Antietam battlefield.
2627	Vermillion, J. K.	"	B	1	Artillery	Aug. 21, 1864	Removed from Frederick
2613	Veith, Bernhard	"	F	10	Infantry	Nov. 25, 1864	"
2729	Vining, James L.	"	A	9	"	Aug. 27, 1864	Removed from Weverton.
2624	Woods, Charles P.	"	G	13	"	Sept. 16, 1864	Removed from Frederick.
2616	West, Hamilton	"	G	5	"	Oct. 13, 1864	"
2715	Wilson, Enos P.	"	K	14	"	Aug. 2, 1864	"
2718	Waters, G. H.	"			"		Removed from Weverton.
2727	Williams, John W.	"	F	13	"	Sept. 12, 1864	"
2759	Wilson, William	"		1	"		Removed from Cumberland.
2845	Warner, William D.	"	A	10	"	Dec. 31, 1862	"
2847	Willey, James A.	"	H	1	"	Feb. 22, 1862	"
2855	Wilson, Joseph C.	"	B	12	"	Dec. 26, 1862	"
2888	Welsh, Thomas S.	"	C	3	Cavalry	May 5, 1865	Blacksmith. Removed from Clarysville.
2884	Warner, John F.	"	A	10	Infantry	Dec. 23, 1862	Removed from Cumberland.

DESCRIPTIVE LIST.

No.	Name	Rank	Co.	Regt.	Arm	Date	Year	Remarks
2876	Willis, Francis M.	Private	A	3	Cavalry,	June 15,	1865	Removed from Clarysville.
2875	Wymer, John	"	M	3	"	Oct. 9,	1864	"
2872	Willis, George W.	"	E	5	Infantry,	Mar. 21,	1865	"
2949	Wildman, Henry	"	E	3	Cavalry,	May 19,	1865	"
2748	Yost, John N.	"	C	7	Infantry,			Removed from Cumberland.

WISCONSIN.

No.	Name	Rank	Co.	Regt.	Arm	Date	Year	Remarks
3350	Alexander, John	Corporal,	A	6	Infantry,	Sept. 17,	1862	Killed in action. Removed from Antietam.
3341	Abbott, Charles A.	Private,	K	6	"	Sept. 17,	1862	"
3333	Atwood, George W.	"	I	6	"	Sept. 17,	1862	"
3224	Anders, Ignatius	"	B	2	"	Sept. 17,	1862	"
3228	Allyn, Henry A.	"	H	2	"	Sept. 26,	1862	Died at Frederick.
3250	Artridge, Richard	Corporal,	A	16	"	Sept. 14,	1862	Removed from Antietam.
3212	Allison, Alexander	Private,	A	3	"	Mar. 17,	1862	Removed from Frederick.
3347	Bailey, William	"	H	6	"	Sept. 17,	1862	Killed in action. Rem'd from Antietam.
3335	Brunson, Elie	"	B	7	"	Sept. 17,	1862	
3300	Bridge, Wellington	"	E	2	"	Sept. 17,	1862	Killed at S. Mountain. Rem'd f'm Antietam.
3289	Briggs, James	"	E	7	"	Sept. 18,	1862	Died of wounds. Removed from Antietam.
3239	Black, William P.	"	A	6	"	Sept. 17,	1862	Killed in action. Removed from Antietam.
3231	Burbank, D. C.	"	C	6	"	Oct.	1862	Died of wounds received at Middletown, Md.*
3255	Braithwaite, Wilson	"	E	5	"	Oct. 29,	1862	Died of disease at Hagerstown, Md.*
3261	Bentley, Van R.	"	G	2	"	Sept. 20,	1862	Died of wounds received at Antietam.*
3281	Buxton, George	"	I	3	"	Oct. 18,	1861	Removed from Frederick.
3214	Bemis, Joseph W.	"	C	3	"	Dec. 21,	1861	Died at Frederick. Removed from Frederick.
3210	Batchem, Elie D.	"	E	5	"	Dec. 11,	1864	Died at Cumberland. Rem'd f'm Clarysville.
3216	Clark, Austin	"	C	3	"	Nov. 14,	1861	Removed from Frederick.
3343	Casporas, William J.	"	B	6	"	Sept. 17,	1862	Killed in action. Removed from Antietam.
3340	Cummings, Daniel	"	K	6	"	Sept. 17,	1862	"
3339	Cole, Volney A.	"	B	6	"	Sept. 17,	1862	"
3334	Craig, Wesley	"	F	7	"	Sept. 17,	1862	"
3299	Conner, Timothy	"	E	2	"	Sept. 17,	1862	"
3242	Clark, James A.	"	F	7	"	Sept. 14,	1862	Killed at South Mountain.
3243	Cowley, George W.	"	F	7	"	Sept. 14,	1862	Killed at Antietam.
3247	Cole, Rufus	"	B	7	"	Oct. 7,	1852	Died of wounds.
3269	Chestnut, Jasper N.	Sergeant,	C	6	"	Jan. 23,	1863	Died at Frederick of disease.

* Removed from Antietam.

120   ANTIETAM NATIONAL CEMETERY.

WISCONSIN—CONTINUED.

Headst'e No.	NAME	Rank	Company	Regim't	Arm of Service	Date of Death		REMARKS
3283	Clement, Henry	Private,	A	3	Infantry,	Oct. 16,	1861	Killed in action. Rem'd from Frederick.
3215	Close, Levi	"	D	3	"	Jan. 25,	1862	Removed from Frederick.
3349	Douglass, George	"	L	6	"	Sept. 17,	1862	Killed in action. Rem'd from Antietam.
3359	Drake, George C.	"	A	1	"	July 2,	1861	Killed at Falling Waters, Va.†
3270	Dean, Jesse P.	"	B	3	"	Feb. 5,	1863	Died of disease at Frederick, Md.*
3303	Elterman, Gustave	"	G	2	"	Sept. 17,	1862	Killed in action. Rem'd from Antietam.
3264	Eagan, John	"	D	6	"	Oct. 10,	1862	Died of wounds at Frederick, Md.*
3272	Ellis, J. H.	"	F	7	"	April 7,	1862	Age 21—Died of disease.*
3296	Flanagan, Vincent	"	E	2	"	Sept. 29,	1862	Killed in action. Rem'd from Antietam.
3240	Fletcher, Theodore	"	G	6	"	Sept. 21,	1862	Died of wounds. "
3235	Fox, William	Sergeant,	L	6	"	Oct. 15,	1862	Died of wounds. Rem'd from Smoketown.
3263	Frodinc, John W.	Private,	G	3	"	Sept. 19,	1862	Died of wounds at Frederick.*
3285	Folts, Richard	"	L	6	"	Sept. 17,	1862	Killed in action. Removed from Frederick.
3351	Geary, Francis	"	D	6	"	Sept. 17,	1862	" Removed from Antietam.
3344	Gluth, Frederick	"	B	6	"	Sept. 17,	1862	"
3316	Glasur, Frederick	1st Serg't,	A	3	"	Oct. 26,	1852	Died of wounds.
3238	Gerlongh, Frank	Private,	A	6	"	Sept. 17,	1862	Killed in action.
3258	Geisel, Edward	"	C	5	"	Dec. 7,	1862	Died of disease at Hagerstown, Md.*
3275	Gilbert, George	"	F	2	"	Sept. 14,	1862	Killed at S. Mountain. Rem'd f'm Antietam.
3278	Gaston, John T.	"	F	3	"	Nov. 30,	1861	Died in Frederick.
3221	Gallop, Henry	"	K	3	"	Feb. 16,	1862	"
3266	Gee, J. W.	"	C	2	"	Oct. 28,	1862	Removed from Antietam.
3301	Halloway, George W.	Corporal,	H	2	"	Sept. 17,	1862	Killed in action. Removed from Antietam.
3398	Heise, Frederick	Private,	H	2	"	Sept. 26,	1862	Died of wounds. "
3288	Hamilton, Arthur T.	Corporal,	K	2	"	Sept. 17,	1862	Killed in action.
3336	Harrison, William P.	Private,	L	6	"	Sept. 17,	1862	Killed in action. Removed from Smoketown.
3345	Harding, John	"	F	7	"	Nov. 18,	1862	Died of wounds at Boonsboro', Md.*
3248	Halbert, George F.	Corporal,	B	7	"	Sept. 29,	1862	Died of wounds at Middletown, Md.*
3253	Hancock, Edwin R.	"	B	7	"	Sept. 20,	1862	" "
3267	Hubbard, Howard A.	Private,	A	5	"	Nov. 4,	1862	Died in Frederick.

* Removed from Antietam.   † First man killed in action in a Wisconsin regiment in the late war.

DESCRIPTIVE LIST.

No.	Name	Rank	Co.	Regt.	Date	Year	Remarks
3218	Hoage, Lewis S.	Private,	I	3 Infantry,	Jan. 12,	1862	Died in Fred'k. accident. Rem'd f'm Fred'k.
3345	Islep, George	Corporal,	F	"	Sept. 17,	1862	Killed in action. Removed from Antietam.
3327	Johns, Joshua P.	Private,	H	"	Sept. 17,	1862	" "
3324	Johnson, Emmet J.	Corporal,	K	"	Sept. 17,	1862	" "
3256	Jones, Moses W.	Private,	H	"			Removed from Antietam.
3211	Johnson, John Chris.	"	K	"	April 25,	1862	Died at Frederick. Removed from Frederick.
3346	Koffler, Joseph	"	H	"	Sept. 17,	1862	Killed in action. Removed from Antietam.
3336	Kuntz, Lewis	"	F	"	Sept. 17,	1862	" "
3295	Knutson, Thomas	Corporal,	H	"	Sept. 17,	1862	" "
3229	Kline, William	Private,	H	"	Sept. 29,	1862	Died of wounds at Keedysville, Md.‡
3231	Knutsen, Isaac	"	H	"	Oct. 10,	1862	Died of disease. Rem'd from Smoketown.
3253	Keeler, Amos D.	"	D	"	Oct. 7,	1862	Died of wounds. Removed from Smoketown.
3240	Kaump, Henry A.	"	F	"	Sept. 14,	1862	Killed at S. Mountain. Rem'd f'm Antietam.
3329	Last, Ferdinand	"	D	"	Sept. 17,	1862	Killed in action. Removed from Antietam.
3234	Link, David H.	"	C	"	Oct. 28,	1862	Died of disease. Rem'd from Smoketown.
3223	Limkins, J. A.	"	E	"	Oct. 9,	1862	Frederick.
3348	McCawdron, Martin	"	B	"	Sept. 17,	1862	Killed in action. Removed from Antietam.
3319	Magloskey, Frederick	"	B	"	Sept. 20,	1862	Died of wounds. " "
3317	McIntosh, Lachlin L.	"	E	"	Sept. 17,	1862	Killed in action.
3297	McKenzie, R. Harrison	"	C	"	Sept. 26,	1862	Died of wounds.
3227	McKinney, William G.	"	C	"	Sept. 23,	1862	
3237	Moore, Joseph M.	Corporal,	G	"	Oct. 19,	1862	Died of wounds at Boonsboro', Md.*
3244	Marks, John L.	Private,	F	"	Sept. 14,	1862	Killed at S. Mountain. Rem'd f'm Antietam.
3273	McHardy, Harmon	"	B	"	Mar. 30,	1863	Age 32—Died of disease. Rem'd f'm Ant'm.
3284	Mosier, S. E.	"	C	"	Oct. 16,	1861	Killed in action. Removed from Frederick.
3220	Meyers, John	"	D	"	Nov. 17,	1861	Died of disease. Removed from Frederick.
3213	Matte, Charles	"	E	"	July 6,	1862	Died of wounds received at Winchester, Va.†
3313	Neaville, Henry B.	"	C	"	Sept. 17,	1862	Removed from Antietam.
3277	Noricond, Israel M.	Corporal,	L	"	Dec. 16,	1861	Age 52—Died of disease.
3222	Nelson, William A.	Private,	C	"	Oct. 16,	1862	Removed from South Mountain.
3271	Newcomb, W. B.	"		"	Mar. 5,	1863	Removed from Frederick.
3217	Northrup, Horace	"		"			Removed from Antietam.
3335	Oleson, John	Corporal,	F	"	Sept. 17,	1862	Killed in action. Rem'd from Antietam.
3314	Olin, Uriel P.	Private,	B	"	Sept. 17,	1862	
3352	Osborn,						
3260	Osborn, Charles D.	Corporal,	G	"	Nov. 24,	1862	Died at Hagerstown of disease.‡
3274	Ordway, Benjamin P.	"	D	"	Oct. 3,	1862	Died at Frederick of wounds.‡

* Removed from Smoketown.   † Removed from Frederick.   ‡ Removed from Antietam.

WISCONSIN—CONTINUED.

Head'st'e No.	NAME.	Rank.	Company	Regime't	Arm of Service.	Date of Death.		REMARKS.
3287	Osmundson, Ole	Private,	K	3	Infantry,	Oct. 17,	1861	Died at Frederick of disease.†
3306	Pardee, Marcus	"	A	2	"	Sept. 17,	1862	Killed in action. Rem'd from Antietam.
3246	Pierce, Hiram	"	A	7	"	Oct. 17,	1862	Died of wounds at Middletown, Md.‡
3279	Pierce, Erwin	"	H	3	"	Oct. 30,	1861	Died at Fred'k. Removed from Antietam.
3305	Reibe, Ferdinand	"	B	2	"	Sept. 17,	1862	Killed in action. Rem'd from Antietam.
3257	Rath, Charles	"	A	5	"	Nov. 8,	1862	Died at Hagerstown of disease.‡
3276	Remmele, John	"	K	3	"	Sept. 24,	1861	Died at Frederick of disease.‡
3286	Raymond, Henry	"	C	3	"	Oct. 16,	1861	Killed in action. Rem'd from Frederick.
3337	Sawyer, J. D.	"	A	7	"	Sept. 17,	1862	Removed from Antietam.
3332	Sutter, Nicholas	"	B	6	"	Sept. 17,	1862	"
3331	Sargent, Gustavus	Corporal,	E	7	"	Sept. 17,	1862	"
3315	Snyder, Edwin R.	Private,	D	3	"	Sept. 27,	1862	Died of wounds.
3302	Stevenson, R. S.	"	C	2	"	Sept. 17,	1862	Killed in action.
3225	Storm, Henry	"	"	"	"	Sept. 17,	1862	"
3262	Smith, Henry	Sergeant,	H	2	"	Oct. 16,	1862	Removed from Antietam.
3280	Steigman, John	Corporal,	K	2	"	Oct. 28,	1861	Died of disease. Removed from Frederick.
3320	Stansbury, William	Private,	B	3	"	Sept. 17,	1862	Killed in action. "
3338	Tapping, John	"	I	3	"	Sept. 17,	1862	Killed in action. Rem'd from Antietam.
3330	Thurlow, Isaac	"	—	7	"	Sept. 17,	1862	Killed in action. "
3326	Temple, J. L.	"	C	3	"	Sept. 17,	1862	"
3322	Talbott, W. H.	"	D	3	"	Sept. 17,	1862	"
3318	Tait, Henry H.	"	—	2	"	Sept. 17,	1862	Died of wounds.
3226	Taplin, Osman B.	"	G	3	"	Sept. 24,	1862	Removed from Antietam.
3282	Tuttle, Lorenzo F.	"	E	2	"	Oct. 16,	1861	Died of wounds. Rem'd from Antietam.
3290	Waterhouse, M. J.	"	A	3	"	Unknown,		Killed in action. Removed from Frederick.
3328	Wilcox, William	"	H	3	"	Sept. 17,	1862	Killed in action. Removed from Antietam.
3323	White, Thomas A.	"	—	3	"	Sept. 17,	1862	"
3321	Wescott, Charles	"	—	3	"	Sept. 21,	1862	Died of wounds.
3232	Weber, George	"	E	3	"	Sept. 10,	1862	" Removed from Smoketown.
3249	Wheeler, Edwin	"	B	7	"	Sept. 17,	1862	Killed in action. Removed from Antietam.

† Removed from Frederick.   ‡ Removed from Antietam.

DESCRIPTIVE LIST.   123

3265	Weber, Peter	Private,	H	6 Infantry,	Oct. 23,	1862	Died at Frederick, of wounds.*
3268	Wilcox, Daniel	"	G	7 "	Oct. 28,	1862	Died at Middletown. Rem'd from Antietam.
3342	Young, David Z.	Corporal,	B	6 "	Sept. 17,	1862	Killed in action. Removed from Antietam.
3304	Yates, John	"	F	2 "	Sept. 17,	1862	"
3219	Varger, Perry L.	Private,	C	3 "	Nov. 26,	1861	Died at Frederick. Removed from Frederick. Removed from Antietam.
12 Unknown—Wisconsin.							

* Removed from Antietam.

UNITED STATES REGULARS.

3507	Anderson, Joseph	Private,	A	1 Cavalry,	Sept. 7,	1862	Removed from Weverton.
3515	Boles, William	"	B	6 "	Nov. 9,	1862	Removed from Burkettsville.
3540	Balden, Francis	"	G	4 Artillery,	Oct. 23,	1862	Removed from Frederick.
3546	Berghauser, August	"	B	4 Infantry,	Dec. 6,	1862	"
3563	Blal, John	"	M	2 Cavalry,	Oct. 11,	1863	Age 18—Removed from Frederick.
3580	Baker, J. S.	"	F	4 Artillery,	Mar. 12,	1862	Removed from Frederick.
3574	Bale, J. G.	"	E	5 Cavalry,			Removed from Cumberland.
3516	Carrigan, James	"		17			Removed from South Mountain.
3510	Cooper, William	"	D	2 "	Oct. 25,	1864	Removed from Weverton.
3497	Connolly, Thomas	"	M	5 "			Removed from Hagerstown.
3538	Casey, Richard	"	G	4 Infantry,	Oct. 23,	1862	Removed from Frederick.
3559	Carr, Michael	"	B	2 Cavalry,	July 6,	1863	"
3566	Christian, Leon	"	L	1 Artillery	Sept. 7,	1863	Age 23—Removed from Frederick.
3570	Clehane, J.	"	B	11 Infantry	Sept. 17,	1862	Removed from Frederick.
3548	Drinkwater, George	"	E	12 "	Nov. 2,	1862	"
4232	Dellinger, John	"		4 U. S. Artillery,			Removed from Hagerstown. Dec. 1889.
3545	Erichsen, Peter	Sergeant,	F	2 Artillery,	Dec. 8,	1862	Removed from Frederick.
3519	Finley, William	Private,	M	"	Sept. 17,	1862	Removed from Antietam battlefield.
3503	Funk, William	"	E	4 "			Age 22—Removed from Sandy Hook.
3551	Foley, Morgan	"	H	14 "	Nov. 29,	1862	Removed from Frederick.
3552	Ford, James	"	C	12 Infantry,	Dec. 24,	1863	"
3556	Filkins, Anthony	"	E	14 "	Jan. 1,	1863	"
3560	French, C. R.	"	K	1 Artillery,	July 13,	1863	Age 19—Removed from Frederick.
3525	Glessner, Philip	"		12 "			Removed from Antietam battlefield.
3518	Griffin, Timothy	"	G	5 Cavalry,	Aug. 31,	1864	Removed from South Mountain.
3508	Hutchings, F. M.	"	C	Artillery,			Removed from Weverton.
3504	Hickey, Peter	"		2 Infantry,			Removed from Antietam battlefield.

UNITED STATES REGULARS—Continued.

Hends't No.	NAME	Rank	Company	Regim't	Arm of Service	Date of Death		REMARKS
3555	Harris, James	Private,	B	12	Infantry,	Dec. 24,	1862	Removed from Frederick
3567	Hall, Jared	"	B	5	Artillery,	Jan. 15,	1864	" [in Pittsfield, Mass.
3531	Jones, Calvin	"		11				Age 25—Rem'd f'm Ant'm battlefield. Born
3498	Kenouse, L. J.	"	F	2	Cavalry,	Mar. 19,	1865	Removed from Hagerstown.
3542	Kelley, James	"	B	9	"	Oct. 22,	1862	Removed from Frederick.
3565	Kelly, Levi	"	D	6	"	Sept. 1,	1863	Age 22—Removed from Frederick.
3568	Kelly, Michael J.	"	D	1	"	Mar. 22,	1865	Removed from Frederick.
3522	McCaffery, Charles	"	L	6	"	Sept. 17,	1862	Removed from Antietam battlefield.
3520	Meyer, Adolph	Sergeant,	B	1	"	July 11,	1863	"
3505	McConnell, William	Private,	F	5	Artillery,			Removed from Hagerstown.
3549	Marsh, Albert N.	"	G	17	"	Dec. 1,	1862	Removed from Frederick.
3554	Mills, Thomas B.	"	E	6	Infantry,	Jan. 5,	1863	"
3564	McCann, Samuel	"	F	1	Cavalry,	Aug. 10,	1863	Age 24—Removed from Frederick.
3571	McGuire, Michael	"	C	4	Infantry,	Sept. 30,	1862	Removed from Frederick.
3572	Mitchell, Samuel	"		12	"	Oct. 6,	1862	"
3581	McCann, William J.	"	F	4	Artillery,	Mar. 15,	1862	"
3579	McDermott, James	"	F		"	Apr. 10,	1862	"
3576	Maier, John	"	B	3	"	Aug. 13,	1865	Removed from Clarysville.
3535	Oliver, John H.	Corporal,	K	4	Cavalry,	July		Removed from Funkstown.
3524	O'Dowd, James	"		5	"			Removed from Antietam battlefield.
3557	Olcott, Harrison	"	E	7	Infantry,	July 4,	1863	Removed from Frederick.
3513	Parsons, Henry	Private,	H	1	Cavalry,			Removed from Weverton.
3532	Ransom, J. H.	"		12	"			Removed from Antietam battlefield.
3530	Robinson, Robert I.	"	C	6	Musician,			"
3521	Rourk, John	"	C	4	Infantry,	Sep. 17,	1862	Removed from South Mountain.
3517	Rockwell, P.	"	B	12	"	Sep. 21,	1862	"
3562	Reed, C. B.	"	B	17	"			Age 26—Removed from Frederick.
3573	Rice, Edward W.	"	4	1	Battaillon,	Aug. 28,	1863	Vet. Res. Corps. Removed from Clarysville.
3533	Sumner, A. P.	"	C	12	Cavalry,	Oct. 20,	1862	Removed from Antietam battlefield.
3511	Smith, Charles L.	"	B	2	"	Sep. 11,	1864	"
3509	Schlichter, Jacob	"		5	"	Aug. 1,	1864	Removed from Weverton.

DESCRIPTIVE LIST.

3536	Shaughnassey, John	Private,	G	8 Infantry,	Oct. 14, 1862	Removed from Frederick.
3541	Sumner, Lewis S.	"	B	17 "	Oct. 31, 1862	"
3543	Schmitt, Julius	"	L	5 Artillery,	Nov. 1, 1862	"
3544	Schenck, Mabury	"	K	5 "	Dec. 9, 1862	"
3547	Smith, Adelbert	"	D	14	Nov. 4, 1862	"
3550	Spix, Bernard	"	H	12	Nov. 29, 1862	"
3569	Simon, Jacob	"	L	5 Cavalry,	Mar. 15, 1865	"
3575	Sendner, Philip	"	B	5 Artillery,	July 30, 1864	Removed from Clarysville.
3537	Seipe, William	"	A	14 Cavalry,	Oct. 23, 1862	Removed from Frederick.
3523	Tucker, A. W.					Removed from Antietam battlefield.
3539	Thesaug, H. T.	"	C	3 Artillery,	Oct. 29, 1862	Removed from Frederick.
3553	Thayer, Horace P.	"	D	3 Infantry,	Jan. 12, 1863	Removed from Clarysville.
3577	Taylor, Charles D.	"	A	5 Cavalry,	Nov. 2, 1864	Removed from Antietam battlefield.
3529	Unknown,	"		12		"
3528	"	"		12		"
3527	"	"		12		"
3526	"	"		12		Removed from Weverton.
3506	"	"		12		Removed from Hagerstown.
3502	"	"		8 Infantry,		"
3500	"	"		12 Infantry, Cavalry,		Removed from Antietam battlefield.
3534	Woodcock, Selvey H.	"	C	2 Cavalry,	Oct. 20, 1862	Age 31—Removed from Brownsville.
3514	Weiser, Andrew	"	E	1 Artillery		Removed from Weverton.
3512	White, Edward	"		8 Infantry,		Rem'd from Hagerstown. Capt. Frank's Co.
3501	Whitington, John	"	D	2 Artillery,		
3499	Walker, E. R.	"	K	1 "	July 8, 1863	Age 24—Removed from Frederick.
3558	Wooster, W. S.	Corporal,	H	"	July 9, 1863	Age 30—Removed from Frederick.
3561	Waldin, L. F.	Private,		Signal Corps,	Nov. 15, 1864	Removed from Clarysville.
3578	Williams, Clark					

VERMONT.

2656	Baker, Jacob	Private,	K	9 Infantry,	Oct. 23, 1864	Age 50—Removed from Weverton.
2655	Bean, Albert	"	D	2 "	Oct. 4, 1864	Age 23—Removed from Weverton.
2648	Bartlett, Marston H.	"	D	4 "	Aug. 25, 1863	Age 18—Removed from Frederick.
2637	Blodgett, Jackson	"	I	11 "	Dec. 1, 1864	Age 29— "
2634	Burnes, James, Jr.	"		1 Cavalry,	Sept. 30, 1864	Unassigned for 1st Veteran Cavalry.
2633	Beals, James M.	"		1 "	Jan. 8, 1865	"

VERMONT—Continued.

Headst'e No.	NAME.	Rank.	Company	Regiment	Arm of Service.	Date of Death.			REMARKS.
2666	Bates, George F.	Private,	M	1	Artillery,	Aug.	27,	1864. Age 18—	Removed from Antietam.
2677	Briggs, Sylvester F.	"	A	4	Infantry,	Nov.	13,	1862 Age 18—	Removed from Hagerstown.
2635	Cunningham, Robert T.	"	K	"	"	Oct.	9,	1864 Age 32—	Removed from Frederick.
2693	Cross, Nelson N.	"	C	5	Cavalry,	July	10,	1863 Age 18—	Removed from Funkstown.
2658	Dean, Simon P.	"	C	5	Infantry,	Aug.	24,	1864 Age 32—	Removed from Weverton.
2657	Day, William H.	"	H	1	Cavalry,	Aug.	25,	1864 Age 18—	"
2652	Delhanty, Patrick	"	F	14	Infantry,	July	17,	1863 Age 19—	Removed from Frederick.
2668	Davidson, David B.	Corporal,	L	6	"	Nov.	5,	1862 Age 19—	Removed from Hagerstown.
2671	Everest, George W.	Sergeant,	E	1	Cavalry,	July	14,	1863 Age 18—	Removed from Williamsport.
2651	Fales, Albert E.	Private,	K	3	Infantry,	Sept.	21,	1864 Age 43—	Removed from Weverton.
2660	Fay, Emmerson C.	"	D	10	"	Sept.	24,	1864 Age 19—	"
2669	Ford, Charles	Corporal,	D	3	"	Dec.	22,	1862 Age 21—	Died in Court-house, Hagerstown.
2640	Gray, Alva M.	Private,	D	6	"	Sept.	17,	1864 Age 32—	Removed from Frederick.
2647	Holmes, Lyman B.	"	K	3	"	Nov.	1,	1862 Age 20—	"
2676	Horner, Albert N.	"	L	10	"	Nov.	19,	1862 Age 31—	Removed from Hagerstown.
2641	Hopkins, Patrick	"	C	"	"	Aug.	7,	1864 Removed from Frederick.	
2658	Hall, Theodore H.	"	E	4	"	Aug.	12,	1864 Age 23—	Removed from Frederick.
2674	Hoose, Sylvester J.	"	K	3	"	Nov.	24,	1862 Age 22—	Removed from Hagerstown.
2679	Hathaway, Calvin	"	A	2	"	Nov.	23,	1862 Age 18—	"
2672	Kimball, George H.	"		1	"			Removed from Williamsport.	
2663	Ladam, Peter	"	A	5	"	Aug.	22,	1864 Age 18—	Removed from Weverton.
2651	Lackie, Marvin H.	"	K	6	"	Oct.	24,	1863 Age 18—	Removed from Frederick.
2645	Locklin, Dennis	"	C	10	"	July	12,	1864 Age 33—	"
2636	Late, David	"	K	1	Cavalry,	Jan.	2,	1865 Age 19—	"
2675	Lane, Noah L.	"	D	4	Infantry,	Nov.	14,	1852 Removed from Hagerstown.	
2692	Leonard, J. W.	Sergeant,		5	Cavalry,	July		1863 Removed from Frederick.	
2665	Morse, Isaac E.	"		3	"			Removed from Antietam battlefield.	
2613	Marson, Joseph	Private,	H	4	Infantry,	Sept.	15,	1861 Age 25—	Removed from Frederick.
2673	Maloney, Michael	"	H	3	"	Nov.	21,	1862 Age 21—	Removed from Hagerstown.
2680	Musk, Edward D.	"	K	10	"	Oct.	2,	1864 Age 24—	Removed from Frederick.
2689	Madigo, Henry H.	Corporal,	I	2	"	Oct.	15,	1862 Age 27—	Removed from Hagerstown.

DESCRIPTIVE LIST.

2697	Muntz, John	Private,	B	10 Infantry,	Feb. 23, 1862	Removed from Cumberland.
2650	Page, Hiram T.	"	K	15 "	July 23, 1863 Age 23—	Removed from Frederick.
2649	Page, Alvah G.	"	F	3 "	July 22, 1863 Age 21—	"
2644	Parsons, Edwin W.	"	A	1 Artillery,	Aug. 11, 1864 Age 19—	
2694	Partridge, George M.	"	D	6 Infantry,	June 10, 1863 Age 22—	Removed from Funkstown.
2664	Remington, George R.	"	B	14 "	July 19, 1863 Age 19—	Removed from Middletown.
2653	Richardson, George C.	"	H	6 "	Dec. 8, 1862 Age 19—	Removed from Frederick.
2667	Racey, Giles	"	C	5 "	Nov. 26, 1862 Age 21—	Removed from Hagerstown.
2642	Sumner, Samuel W.	Sergeant,	G	8 "	Aug. 5, 1864 Age 40—	Removed from Frederick.
2639	Smith, Alexander	Private,	L	1 Artillery,	Oct. 22, 1864 Age 37—	
2670	Scott, George	"	B	6 Infantry,	Nov. 4, 1862 Age 21—	Removed from Hagerstown.
2678	Sprague, George	"	K	5 "	Nov. 13, 1862 Age 20—	"
2681	Slack, Charles D.	"	G	8 "	Mar. 16, 1865 Age 33—	Removed from Frederick.
2682	Spring, John A.	"		Teamster,	Feb. 22, 1862	Removed from Frederick.
2683	Smith, Royal	"	G	4 Infantry,	Nov. 24, 1862 Age 21—	Removed from Hagerstown.
2662	Turner, Burton C.	"	D	2 "	Nov. 5, 1864 Age 18—	Removed from Weverton.
2654	Thomas, George S.	"	E	11 Cavalry,	Aug. 25, 1864	Removed from Weverton.
2659	Walker, William A.	"	I	3 Infantry,	Aug. 4, 1864 Age 37—	Removed from Weverton.
2684	Watts, Wesley	"	E	1 Cavalry,	July 6, 1863 Age 18—	Removed from Hagerstown.
9	Unknown—Vermont.					Rem'd from Hagerstown and Funkst'wn, Md.

1,436 Unknown U. S. Soldiers.

ANTIETAM NATIONAL CEMETERY.

Number of Section	STATE.	Known.	Unknown.	Total.	REMOVED FROM
16	Connecticut,	80	5	85	Clarysville, Hancock, Frederick, Hagerstown, Weverton and Antietam battle-field.
8	Delaware,	28		28	Frederick, Smoketown Hospital and Antietam battlefield.
7	Illinois,	28	1	29	Boonesboro', Cumberland, Frederick, South Mountain and Antietam battlefield.
22	Indiana,	138	8	146	Clarysville, Cumberland, Frederick, Middletown and Antietam battlefield.
6	Iowa,	2		2	Frederick and Weverton.
9	Maine,	88	8	96	Frederick, Weverton, Smoketown Hospital and Antietam battlefield.
19	Maryland,	87	6	93	Clear Spring, Boonesboro', Frederick, Smoket'n Hosp. and Antietam battlefield.
17	Massachusetts,	130	62	192	Clarysv'e, Fred'k, Hagerst'n, Weverton, Smoketown Hosp. and Ant'm battlefield.
18	Michigan,	100	37	137	Clarysville, Weverton, Frederick, S. Mountain, Smoket'n and Ant'm battlefield.
5	Minnesota,	10		10	Williamsport, Frederick and Antietam battlefield.
12	New Hampshire,	24	1	25	Frederick, Weverton, Middletown and Antietam battlefield
11	New Jersey,	65	5	70	Frederick, Weverton, Hagerstown, Burkettsville and Antietam battlefield.
25	New York,	730	137	867	Keedysv'e, Oldt'n, Hancock, Frederick, Hagerst'n, Weverton, Burkettsv'e, Middlet'n, S. Mount'n,Westernport, Brownsv'e, Smoket'n Hosp. and Antietam battlefield.
23	Officers—(Commissioned,	31	7	38	Frederick, Weverton, Middletown and Antietam battlefield.
1	Ohio,	320	29	349	Clarysv'e,Cumberl'd,Fred'k,Weverton, Middlet'n, S. M't'n and Ant'm battlefield.
26	Pennsylvania,	550	92	644	Clarysv'e, Fred'k, Hagerst'n, S. Mount'n, Smoket'n Hoso. and Ant'm battlefield.
13	Rhode Island,	22	1	23	Frederick, Smoketown and Antietam battlefield.
14 & 20	West Virginia,	171	2	173	Clarysv'e, Cumberland, Fred'k,Weverton, Smoket'n Hosp. and Ant'm battlefield.
10	Wisconsin,	130	12	142	Frederick, Smoketown Hospital and Antietam battlefield.
24	United States Regulars,	79	7	86	Clarysville, Frederick, Hagerst'n. Weverton, S. Mount'n and Antie'm battlefield
21	Vermont,	56	9	65	Funkstown, Frederick, Hagerstown, Weverton and Antietam battlefield.
2,3,4 & 15	Unknown U. S. Soldiers,		1436		Middletown, Burkettsville, Weverton, Smoketown, Hagerstown, Frederick, &c., and Antietam battlefield.
	Grand Total,	2869	1865	4734	

At the commencement of the fiscal year, July 1st, 1889, there were 82 National Cemeteries in the United States. In these Cemeteries repose the remains of 326,391 Union soldiers. Of this number 177,527 are known and 148,864 are unknown.

JUST NOW IS THE TIME TO SUBSCRIBE FOR

The Volunteer,

A Monthly Journal devoted to perpetuating the memory of the Soldiers of the War of the Rebellion. It contains reliable history, biography, gems of poetry, songs with music. Just what is needed to inspire the young with patriotism.

Price, 5 Cts. per Copy. 50 Cts. per Year.

Canvassers Wanted. Address the Editor and Publisher.

J. C. STEVENSON,

NEW CASTLE, PA.

THE

Antietam Battle-Field Guide

Will be sent by mail, Free of Postage, to any address in the United States, upon receipt of TWENTY-FIVE CENTS per copy. Special rates to all G. A. R. Posts, by the hundred or more copies.

Address,

GEO. HESS,

Supt. Antietam National Cemetery,

SHARPSBURG, MARYLAND.